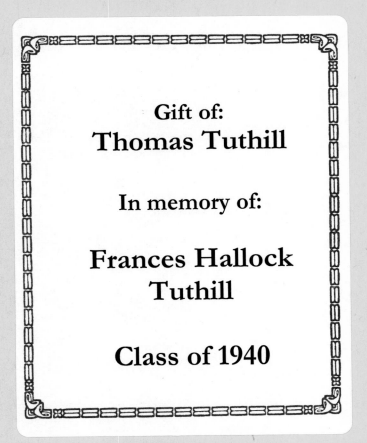

Gift of:
Thomas Tuthill

In memory of:

**Frances Hallock
Tuthill**

Class of 1940

Oberon's Mazéd World

Oberon's Mazéd

T. WALTER HERBERT

Louisiana State University Press / Baton Rouge and London

A Judicious Young Elizabethan
Contemplates *A Midsummer Night's Dream*
World with a Mind
Shaped by
the Learning of Christendom
Modified by the New Naturalist Philosophy
and
Excited by the Vision
of a Rich, Powerful England

Copyright © 1977 by Louisiana State University Press
All rights reserved
Manufactured in the United States of America

Designer: Dwight Agner
Typeface: VIP Trump Mediæval
Typesetter: G&S Typesetters, Inc., Austin, Texas
Printer and binder: Kingsport Press, Kingsport, Tennessee

LIBRARY OF CONGRESS CATALOGING IN PUBLICATION DATA

Herbert, Thomas Walter, 1908–
    Oberon's mazéd world.

    Includes bibliographical references and index.
    1. Shakespeare, William, 1564–1616. Midsummer night's dream.
2. Shakespeare, William, 1564–1616—Contemporary England.
I. Title.
PR2827.H45   822.3'3   77–4082
ISBN 0–8071–0290–3

To
JEAN ELIZABETH
Most high and happy Princess,
I must tell you a tale of a man at a play.

The seasons alter: hoary headed frosts
Fall in the fresh lappe of the Crymson rose,
And on old Hyems chinne and Icy crowne,
An odorous Chaplet of sweete Sommer buddes
Is, as in mockery, set. The Spring, the Sommer,
The childing Autumne, angry Winter change
Their wonted Liveries: and the mazed worlde,
By their increase, now knowes not which is which:
And this same progeny of evils,
Comes from our debate, from our dissention:
We are their Parents and originall.

> —Titania on the Athenian Predicament

Her influence the heaven forbears.

> —John Donne on the Anatomy of the World

I never may beleeve
These antique fables, nor these Fairy toyes.

> —Theseus on Athenian Theology

CONTENTS

ACKNOWLEDGMENTS

I AM TEMPTED to boast the help of all those whose conversation taught me how to approach the nonpoetry books and activities which educated the playgoer I have devised, but I shall name just twenty-one. They have not known I was plundering their minds, and indeed I was not intentionally doing that when I listened to them, but though none of these is mentioned in a note, I am now conscious of a specific debt to each. Eleven are scholars in the University of Florida: for astronomy and physics Alex Smith, for biology Henry Wallbrunn, for chemistry John Baxter, for economics Clement Donovan, for education Vynce Hines, for history Ashby Hammond, for music Reid Poole, for the art of painting Hiram Williams, for philosophy A. L. Lewis, for religion Delton Scudder, for rhetoric Tommy Ruth Waldo. Ten are not in my university: for business enterprise Frank Chadwick of Connecticut and Tom Traywick of South Carolina, for education Philip Eschbach of Brevard Junior College, for the history of science Frank Haber of the University of Maryland, for law Judge R. A. Green, Jr., of Gainesville and Carlisle Herbert of Chicago, for mathematics John Maxfield of Kansas State University, for medicine Dr. Linton Herbert of Baltimore, for music Faye Miles and Muriel Williamson of Gainesville.

The British Museum and the libraries of the University of Florida contain much I ought to have read but have not. Even so, mine is an emphatically bookish book. Emphatic is my gratitude to the people, especially in these two places, who have efficiently, generously, and amiably made book knowledge come readily to hand.

I toast those splendid anonymous people who by condemning earlier efforts enabled me at length to know what I wanted to do. I salute those even more splendid people connected with the Louisiana State University Press who have {xi given welcome for my final version, especially Lloyd Lyman, Beverly Jarrett, and Mary Jane DiPiero.

Four people examined my manuscript in its later stages and offered counsel so excellent that only an opinionated man like me could have failed to follow it all: Sidney Homan and Richard Brantley of the University of Florida; T. Walter Herbert, Jr., of Southwestern University, Georgetown, Texas; and Jean Herbert of Gainesville, Florida.

For a faculty development grant, a summer research grant, a travel grant, and moral support I return thanks to the University of Florida, its Humanities Division, its Graduate School, and its Department of English.

For the greater debts I owe I would fain thank William Shakespeare.

PROLOGUE

Playing, whose end, both at the first and now, was and is, to hold, as 'twere, the mirror up to nature; to show virtue her own feature, scorn her own image, and the very age and body of the time his form and pressure. Now this overdone, or come tardy off, though it make the unskillful laugh, cannot but make the judicious grieve; the censure of the which one must, in your allowance, o'erweigh a whole theatre of others.

—*Hamlet*, III, ii

THIS BOOK offers to endow with a certain thoughtfulness the laughter of people who will look at *A Midsummer Night's Dream* through eyes belonging to well-educated, energetic, philosophically adventurous sixteenth-century English playgoers who wondered how best to think about the world they lived in and how to increase their control. The promise resembles, with differences, Henry Adams' promise that we in the twentieth century may see remarkable things at the Cathedral of Our Lady of Chartres if we look through eyes of thirteenth-century Christians concerned over the destiny of their souls. Listen as he talks about the great window that transfigures the afternoon sun streaming into the nave.

Looking carefully, one discovers at last that this gorgeous combination of all the hues of Paradise contains or hides a Last Judgment.... The churchman is the only true and final judge of his own doctrine, and we neither know nor care to know the facts; but we are as good judges as he of the feeling.... That this blaze of heavenly light was intended, either by the Virgin or by her workmen, to convey ideas of terror or pain, is a notion which the Church might possibly preach, but which we sinners knew to be false in the thirteenth century as well as we know it now. Never in all these seven hundred years has one of us looked up at this rose without feeling it to be Our Lady's promise of Paradise.[1]

We do not take Adams literally, that the Virgin acting as architect designed the cathedral and acting as agent of Providence compels all sinners to respond in the single fashion she determines. Whatever may be said about the Virgin as architect, we know that seven hundred years later German soldiers and American tourists, as sinful as Adams could wish, have looked up at the window without feeling need or promise of any Paradise beyond the immediate moment. Adams' very denial acknowledges that to some people the window has meant terror, as to others it has spoken in the allegory of the wheel, and to still others (Englishmen alert to grave puns) has proclaimed the blessed sun.

We read Adams as we read metaphor. He has so concerted his immense learning that, astonished, we understand ancient devotees rapt into ecstasy by the new cathedral, feel the passionate joy of worshipers now long cold among their ashes. If we look at the luminous window through eyes taught by Adams we may well say grace for good eyesight, lose our sinful hearts to Our Lady's control, and mutter a *Nunc Dimittis* before turning away.

This book makes a promise closer to earth than Adams'. Whereas he invites us to regard the cathedral as the embodiment of the Virgin's design, we shall assume that a ground-treading man, not Thalia for comedy or Urania for cosmology, designed *A Midsummer Night's Dream*. Whereas Adams invites us to fit our minds to a great creating imagination, we shall set ourselves to expand our responsive imaginations. By putting into our minds a set of memories derived from some of the best-known light and heavy books accessible to Elizabethans, we shall imitate memories, attitudes, and responses that belonged to playgoers whom we may call, with Hamlet, "judicious." We shall have nothing directly to do with these people in moments when they joined Adams' sinners in hopes and fears about a Last Judgment and its consequences, for Shakespeare's play summons up no such passions. We shall share the perceptions that belonged to them because they had tinkered, not quite irreverently but most urgently, with cosmic models. They were laughter-prone, book-reading, gregarious, lively people—responsive to Lysander and Bottom, each of whom reaches for control in a world he does not well understand.

Instead of offering a new chapter for a history of great ideas, this book conjures up and follows a representative mind through a few hours in the year 1595 [2]—the mind of a playgoer grounded in the old, reaching for the new, and aware of spiritual tension. By accompanying him we mean to acquire an Elizabethan's understanding of Shakespeare's still delightful comedy.[3] Except for the one fiction of a created persona, we shall observe the boundary of verifiable fact. Some facts important for our purposes reach as far back as Homer. Many have no obvious kinship with one another except in the comedy, where their often distorted forms acquire a wild, dreamlike coherency.

We could not hope to understand a sixteenth-century mentality without the work of earlier scholars. They have reconstructed audiences at Globe and Blackfriars, at Queen Elizabeth's court and noblemen's houses.[4] They have illuminated social conditions, tastes, levels of literacy, moods, habits, and tempers. They have described the classical world, the world of romance, the fairy worlds, the middle-class world, the worlds of orthodox theologians and natural philosophers, and a sweet English countryside.[5]

We shall not imitate critics who like Alexander Pope undertake to read a work "With the same Spirit that its Author writ." They sometimes describe beliefs and purposes that stirred Shakespeare just before he dipped his pen. They write in a tradition exemplified by Theseus, who looks behind the poetry to see the poet, rolling eyes and all. To this great tradition belong Sir Philip Sidney, Samuel Johnson, and John Livingston Lowes.[6]

In contemplating aspects of Shakespeare's comedy we shall imitate Hamlet rather than Theseus. Hamlet did not expect Claudius to assess the artistry of whoever wrote "The Murder of Gonzago." He expected that Claudius' memories and attitudes would determine his responses to the fiction. We do not suppose that the playgoer who interests us was an absolutely detached spectator. He participated in the play as surely as Claudius did, if less disastrously. We need not be sleuths like Hamlet, for printed words tell us plainly what memories belonged to play-goers at early performances of *A Midsummer Night's Dream*. Insofar as we can acquire their intellectual and social readiness, or at least that part of their readiness which the play itself stirred into action, we can claim to look with their eyes.

The audience we shall join contained vigorous people, old and young. There was the learned queen. There were men like Sir Walter Ralegh and the Earl of Essex—lovers passionate as Lysander, but dependable for the briefings that together with books, visitors, and royal progresses kept Elizabeth in touch with her world. There were natural philosophers who clung as tightly as Pyramus, if less naively, to the animist's vision: William Gilbert, John Dee, and Francis Bacon. There were imaginative mathematicians suspected of implying that world forces can be quantified: Thomas Hariot, Thomas Hood, and the Henry Briggs who later did so much with John Napier's logarithms. There were versatile rhetoricians like Gabriel Harvey; lawyers like Sir Edward Coke and residents of the Inns of Court, who delighted in problems of young people wanting to marry against their parents' will; musicians like John Bull, William Byrd, and Thomas Morley, who understood human discords in Pythagorean terminology; clergymen like Richard Hooker and Lancelot Andrewes from the Establishment, for whom social order was a function of divine will; merchants like Thomas Smith, profiting from the new technology and dreaming of the East India Company; star-gazing mathematical navigators like John Davis; and captains like the Lord Admiral Charles Howard, in the tradition of Sir Humphrey Gilbert, Sir Martin Frobisher, Sir Francis Drake, and Sir John Hawkins, who contemplated the weltering sea with an itch as strong as Bottom's for control. Some intelligent and well-informed men, like Lord Burghley, stayed away from plays on principle, but many of the hundreds with whom the great ones could carry on conversation were apt to be found at *A Midsummer Night's Dream*.

The judicious playgoer whom we shall conjure up deserves a modest place in this company. He is a skeptical Cambridge graduate, in whose memory Shakespeare's happy play is fresh and vivid. In order to let him talk with us easily about the play, we shall confer on him a little knowledge about the intervening centuries and the world we live in. But we shall limit his responses to those of which he was demonstrably capable in 1595. He then knew nothing, for instance, of psychoanalysis, sociology, or *The Golden Bough*, nor had he been embittered by a twentieth-century holocaust using end products of a science whose beginnings he regarded with more hope than horror, though with some apprehension too.

This spirit we shall raise is no *Zeitgeist*. A *Zeitgeist* cannot think inductively, but our playgoer could and did, and he made it a point of pride. He had a life history, ideas, and attitudes resembling those that belonged to friends of his whom we have read about. Since his views were a little different from those they held (as they differed from each other) and from yours and mine, he saw a slightly different play. Twenty-seven years old, he had read voraciously in the Bible, in narratives that appealed to the younger sort, in intellectually disturbing ancient and modern philosophies capable of misleading youth, and in other books that he will mention.

In childhood he had heard from his mother and her maids stories of changelings, fairies, and Robin Goodfellow. As a boy he had listened to citizens who fabricated and distributed goods and financed great ventures, especially Sir Thomas Gresham. His father, a prosperous member of the Ironmongers Company, had given him a respect for profits, and he was pleased that by purchasing a coat of arms his father had made him a gentleman born. Not a Puritan like his father, he retained a friendliness for Puritans.

At Cambridge he had met Henry Briggs and acquired an interest in pure and applied mathematics. Intrigued by the doctrines of the pre-Socratics, he had begun to question commonplaces that his parents relied on as they relied on breathing and eating.

Back in London he had found lodging for a few years at Lincoln's Inn. He had formed a friendship with John Donne, whom he knew from before Cambridge; he had gone skylarking, written sonnets, and imagined himself helping to bring about a brave new Athens. He and his kind had provoked greybeards to shake their locks.

Socially adept now, he exploited a knack for engaging active minds in conversation. He frequented places where he could find good talk. He had visited Dr. John Dee's home in Mortlake. He had, so to speak, attended "Sir Walter Rawley's Schoole of Atheisme." He had attended church. Like the friends whose company he relished, he was well known to booksellers on Paul's Walk. He had attended Thomas Hood's lectures. He had visited at the royal palace and at the residences of congenial noblemen. He had junketed to Europe (with a letter from Francis Bacon, the weight of Essex' name behind it) and had broken bread with Galileo Galilei, Tycho Brahe, and strange young Johannes Kepler. He listened best to Bacon himself, who, disenchanted with Cambridge, cultivated philosophical gentlefolk and London citizens.

At Southampton's he had heard Bacon discuss with Will Shakespeare a fascinating consequence of man's fallen nature: the risk of trusting the apparently simple fact that the eyes see, because man tends to see things in the forms that traditional preconceptions impose on events. He had heard Bacon maintain that a proper method of inquiry can give men effective power over nature. To our minds, familiar with P. A. M. Dirac, Werner Heisenberg, René Dubos, and Peter Medawar if not with the laboratory itself, Bacon's celebrated method, even when he had fully developed it, may look quaint when compared with Alfred North Whitehead's phrasing: "Inductive reasoning proceeds from the particular occasion to the particular community of occasions, and from the particular community to relations between particular occasions within that community."[7] But our young friend thought Bacon's conversation profound.

He resented Donne's objection. Induction, said Donne, assembles examples of the obvious, but it provides no starting place for inquiry into debatable matters: sense data are about as reliable as quicksand when one reaches for the truth.

Our young philosopher played games with induction, arriving

at conclusions: his high-born wife had better judgment than other women; English sea captains were more daring than Spanish; the country smelled better than the city; Cantabrigians were abler than Oxonians; colliers cheated noblemen more eagerly than they cheated citizens; large churches were colder in winter than small ones.

When he went to see *A Midsummer Night's Dream* he meant to leave serious thought behind, and in a sense he did. But after two hours he felt that this outrageous play deserves superlatives. The most economically and richly constructed of all cosmic comedies, so he supposed, it addresses exciting questions with insight and gaiety and makes sport of the adventuring mind itself. It brings into one design, in focus for laughter, representative concepts from diverse orders of belief, diverse segments of society, diverse temperaments, and diverse ages of the world's history. It lures one along inductive paths, brings him to the brink of inferences, and then rewards him sometimes with the sense that his imagination has given birth and sometimes with a wry awareness that the birth may be monstrous. With a joy like the joy of scientific discovery he finally understood the Athenian world. The relations he observed between particular occasions within that Athens made provocative sense. From this point to nearly the end of the book we shall listen to his voice.

INTRODUCTION

My library
Was dukedom large enough.
—*The Tempest*, I, ii

M Y FRIENDS and I carried into the theater our dominating interest, human relationships to environments. We expected one kind of behavior at court, another kind in the city, another in the country. Above all, we pored over the book of Nature, speculating about forces that impinge upon man and limit his options. We assumed that people behave in accord with their visions, if any, of God and of spirits abroad in the world.

Our queries about actual environments prepared us to interpret dramatic environments. Before Theseus' first words were many minutes old we began to see a comedy about people in a world complex enough to fascinate a new philosopher. We had noticed that young lovers leave Athens for want of a place for loving and that amateur players leave to seek a place for rehearsal. When we learned that Oberon and Titania had put Athenian seasons out of frame we knew we were observing cosmic matters, determinants of rain and human whim.

School, church, and remembered stories had taught us to interpret unexpected events by looking for celestial antecedents. We knew the argument that regularly repeated motions in nature are evidence of mind, but if minds govern the world, we supposed it possible that minds can change. God's need to prove something to Satan gave meaning to what befell Job, and our own prayers often urged God to change his course. Turbulence in Jove's family gave meaning to what befell Aeneas. And so with no sense of strain we saw Oberon, Titania, Robin, and the tiny fairies simultaneously as characters and as factors in setting: as forces that give distinctive structure and quality to the Athenian world, influencing the behavior of rain and the minds of people.

We entertained more than one concept of nature. Every theological dispute demonstrated that at least one party was wrong in describing ultimate forces. Rival cosmologies were so much in contention that courts indicted men for atheism. Remembering Euclid, Archimedes, and pre-Socratics, we were ready to recognize the dramatic world, devoid of deities, that Quince and his friends display. We were ready to respond to a play imitating people who misconceive their world; who assume they live in one kind when they actually live in another.

We were almost as keenly interested in *how* people think about the world as in what they think. During a conventional, intellectually restful play our mechanisms of understanding no more demanded notice than our eyes did when fascinated by a pretty sight. But we brought to the theater a curiosity about fresh ways of examining, understanding, and controlling nature. Patterns of reasoning that you find unremarkable we sometimes associated with perilous experimentation and naturalist philosophy. Relishing a mildly rebellious thrill every time we studied natural events as anything but expressions of God's mind and will, we were building a readiness to say of Francis Bacon's praise of induction, "Well expressed. Just what I have been thinking." At *A Midsummer Night's Dream* we noticed inductive sequences and then followed them into inferences only in sophisticated ways flattering to our intellectual pride.

Not yet bent to your modern science, we were just beginning to train the passions of our minds to lust after simplicity—after laws expressible in numbers that give man power to calculate but give nature no freedom, no margin, no opportunity for approximation, let alone discretion. We did not yet imagine a sublunary nature infallibly obeying laws, unlike her thinking offspring who make *to err* and *human* synonymous.

Your Newtonian scientist expects nature to reply to his questions in unambiguous, precise equations. He has achieved success when any competent person attacking the problem he has specified must agree that his statement, and only his, speaks in nature's right voice.[1] Material comfort and power are only part of the wealth such scientists have conferred upon you. We were reaching out to become men of that sort. We were participants in the new business, the new philosophy, the new determination to subjugate nature to man.

Late in the seventeenth century, when modern science was dawning, when Englishmen were glorying in René Descartes and Isaac Newton, Samuel Pepys could listen to engineers and members of the Royal Society but could not enjoy our *Midsummer Night's Dream*. Trusting the dogmas of his time, he could not tolerate the play's comic model of a nature full of vagaries or its brief impudent caricature of a whimless naturalist world.

But nowadays, prodded by Albert Einstein and Whitehead, by Heisenberg and Michael Polanyi,[2] your good scientists envision a less absolute world. Though they believe it has an existence, they recognize that their models of that existence smell of their own mortality. They and you long ago quit supposing they think God's thoughts after him.

You can again bear to think of a nature whose behavior can sometimes be described in equations of probability. You can be patient with phenomena that at one moment say "quanta" and the next moment "waves," patient with teasing electrons that never show all their beauty bare. Contemplating celestial light seduced by a black hole into oblivion, you are dreaming impossibilities no mortal ever dared to dream before. Unlike Pepys, you are prepared to respond like sixteenth-century playgoers: our thinking was moving toward a simplicity yours is moving away from. Configurations of problems that beset us sometimes look strange to you, but our uncertainties about man's place in the universe resemble uncertainties of your own.

Your sense of the comic appears now again spacious enough to fit *A Midsummer Night's Dream*. A world that offers alternative pictures of herself makes us all look funny to ourselves when we find we have seen only our own model and scorned those who see any other. You do not always demand that a play confirm your achieved wisdom and vilify the prejudices of other men. Under the two-hour spell of Shakespeare's magnanimous art you can again remember the facts of a grim world and the delusions of a nonangelic human race and contemplate them clearly and affectionately in laughter.

Lawrence Durrell sounds congenial with the sixteenth century when he makes his Justine use the term *prism-sightedness* to suggest that the best truth about an event may be several visions of it seen together. In that spirit I invite you to entertain my understanding of *A Midsummer Night's Dream*. I do not ask you to abandon your prior understandings merely because they may be logically incompatible with ours. Keep them, whether they are original with you or learned perhaps from Dr. Johnson, who could not tolerate some of our tolerances; perhaps from Nevill Coghill, C. L. Barber, David Young, and Jackson Cope;[3] and surely from lively stage and film productions. I also expect you to approach my story with detachment, demanding facts and a decent regard for what makes facts into evidence. Even so, I think you can join us imaginatively in our art of thinking and in our pictures of the world.

Rosemond Tuve, speaking as a reader of catachresis in particular and, by extension, of all our poetry, says, "If I do not supply something not in the word, the poem remains in part unwritten."[4] The question that from the first fascinated me in Shakespeare's comedy was not why it is funny but what is funny and to what end. I found answers in contexts that my memory supplied. Those things are most persistently funny that reminded me of the living people I knew best—what we read, wanted, did, said, believed. For example, I had friends whose refusal to see plain facts sometimes irritated me, and I was anxious about my own perceptiveness. But Lysander's unremitting obtuseness left me neither irritated nor anxious. Though not harmless, it is funny in such a way that it is forgivable. Lysander is not so forgivable as Bottom, but then he is not so funny either.

I implore you to do as I did—think of the play again and again, as a whole, from differing vantage points, with cumulative responses. In later pages, for example, while I am asking you to notice the play's imitations of business mentality and cold philosophy, I hope you may sustain an awareness of the orchestrated dissonance wrought by the sounds of proper names. I hope that even after we have seen witchcraft vanish from Theseus' realm you will, as I did, remember that witching terror and darkness hold just outside the circle of Athenian moonlight.

Part One
The Old Learning

I FROM ATHENS TO THE WOOD AND BACK AGAIN

> To that place, the sharpe Athenian law
> Can not pursue us.
>
> > (I, i, 162–63)
>
> Every Fairy take his gate,
> And each severall chamber blesse,
> Through this palace, with sweete peace.[1]
>
> > (V, i, 423–25)

T O US who were fascinated by speculations about man's total environment, the structurally unifying development in *A Midsummer Night's Dream* occurred not so much in characters as in setting—the world that includes Athens. We remembered that in tragedies like *Antigone* and *Gorboduc* a protagonist's decision determines the health of a realm. When we saw Lysander urging upon Theseus and Egeus a sensible social discipline instead of a mindless routine, we remembered the women in *Lysistrata* attempting to impose their sanity on an Athens. As we followed events in Shakespeare's Athenian world, however, we began to perceive that the world itself is the active force, shaping the Athenians' rebellions even as it undergoes its own change.[2]

We had oscillated between two concepts of history, each concept accounting for the way events on earth and events in the cosmos respond to what Shakespeare's Sonnet 16 calls "this bloody tyrant, Time." As early as Anaximander's description of the birth and death of worlds, time in the Greek or pagan concept eternally and inexorably produces cycles: what now is, has been, and will be again.[3] This model organized our knowledge of mornings, starry nights, seasons, and resemblances of children to parents. It prepared lovers of returning day and springtime to relish a story whose end restores a condition that has suffered disturbance. *A Midsummer Night's Dream* runs a cycle through three sharply different settings. The first long scene and the last are laid in Theseus' palace, in Athens. The second and next-to-last are laid in Quince's house, in Athens. The central scenes are all laid in a wood, near Athens. The play afforded us a sense of completion when eloping lovers are reconciled to the Athens they have fled as intolerable.

I / A Question of Unity

II / The Circle, the Line, and Athenian Society

{3

St. Augustine rejects the merely cyclic concept, maintaining, in the last twelve chapters of the twelfth book of *The City of God*, that God originally planned and inevitably will produce a single far-off end. This, the great Hebrew linear model, was congenial with hope. We knew it well, through prayers, sermons invoking the convenant with Abraham, the Gospel promises, and even the doctrine of God's unpurchased Grace. We were prepared to enjoy a story that leads to a conclusion different from the beginning and answerable to a stimulated sense of need.

Palace, Quince's house, and wood correspond to three environments that identified people: the court, the city,[4] and the countryside. But Englishmen did not live merely on an island. To be sure, we cherished the ideal of an economic and political commonwealth with every individual serving his own purposes while serving his fellow Englishmen and the queen.[5] Nevertheless, most plain men as well as theologians believed that they and England were active parts of an infinite cosmic order responsive to omnipotent God.[6] At *A Midsummer Night's Dream* we saw court people and city people, but in the woodland outside Athens we found no country people. Instead, we met a cluster of fairies who complete the comic cosmic order responsive to a less-than-omnipotent Oberon. Because of what happens in the wood, the cycle of excursion and return emphasized the more momentous linear movement of the Athenian world from unhappy to happy.

In the initial Athens divisions prevail, aged authority disables young love, the ruler conforms to ruthless law, the weather is said to be disastrously bad, and the mentioned gods do nothing. Hermia and Lysander escape. During the great middle of the play the wood looks more and more like a workshop to repair the world. Events there first reveal that the troubles of mortal Athens result from trouble among its immortals. Then Oberon schemes. Despite all blunders he puts his world to rights, filling Bottom with wonder and bringing maturity to Lysander and Demetrius.

The new Athens realizes a humane if lighthearted justice.[7] In

Love's Labour's Lost we had seen love's conquest of a foolish oath and heard Berowne's witty neo-Pauline doctrine: [8]

> For charity itself fulfills the law,
> And who can sever love from charity?
> (I, iii, 364–65)

So also in the last state of Shakespeare's Athens, though error and arrogance remain possible, the things done lawfully are expressions of love. The small immortals, going about their chores in the palace, exhibit one function of a world fit for hope and joy.

Whenever I have thought over this play, even when it has led me to contemplate my own error, my own pain, and my own relationships with a baffling world, my thoughts have been gentled to remember its aspect as a kind-spirited tale of a city that begins in cruelty and ends in mirth. I have, however, sometimes remembered with admiration the lures that drew me, at my age and with my commitment to the new philosophy, to lose myself in fairyland.

In Shakespeare's early audiences I was one of the veteran doubters. Though not so earthbound as Pepys, we doubters were already apt to be put off by John Lyly's brand of wide-eyed wonders. We were prepared to make extempore a brief against any demand that we reexamine our posture in the world. But while we began by resisting, we listened.

III / The Modest Demand and Beguilement into Fairyland

The comedy began with an example of a familiar fashion, which I like to call the modest demand. The modest demand was partly a reaction against serious calls, godly mystery plays, portentous morality plays, and even farces like *Roister Doister* with its dutiful prologue inveighing against the vainglorious. In Lyly's hands the modest demand imitated self-depreciating letters dedicatory. His Prologue to *Endimion* addresses the queen:

Most high and happy Princess, we must tell you a tale of the Man in the Moon, which, if it seem ridiculous for the method, or superfluous for the matter, or for the means incredible, for three faults we can make but one excuse: it is a tale of the Man in the Moon.

It was forbidden in old time to dispute of Chimaera because it was a fiction: we hope in our times none will apply pastimes, because they are fancies; for there liveth none under the sun that knows what to make of the Man in the Moon.[9]

Some authors, perhaps, told the truth when they claimed inconsequentiality. In Shakespeare's play the modest demand encouraged us to sustain our predisposition to disbelief until, laughing, we perceived a world model too diminutive to deserve the unsheathing of argument.[10]

I saw *A Midsummer Night's Dream* as it was presented at a wedding,[11] and its opening moments invited us to make an easy leap, to a fictional wedding whose planned revelry evoked the stately romantic mood we had learned from the Knight's Tale. However, journeymen who saw the play at the Theater, even if they had never read Chaucer, were also ready for Theseus and Hippolyta. They were accustomed to imaginary sojourns in pseudoclassical lands. They remembered the extant Plautus and Terence, the numerous pieces like the Palamon and Arcite plays that were never printed, and such artful productions as George Peele's *Arraignment of Paris* and Lyly's *Campaspe*. They too had come to see a play, and in the first moments they felt no demand for commitment beyond watching an unblushingly artificial play, laid in a familiar, artificial Athens.

The stylized court acquires definition when Theseus agrees that Hermia must wed as her father chooses. What with the ferocious law, accepted by the duke and recognized resentfully but without astonishment by the young people, what with the lovers' recitation that true love must be ever crossed, we knew we were in a storybook land. We were diverted, not revolted. I really was not quite callous. I had sympathized with Juliet's dilemma, and a few years later the sentence pronounced upon tongue-tied Cordelia horrified me. In Lear's world as in Juliet's, people get hurt. The Athenian law announces a gamelike convention, not a persuasive cruelty. It encouraged me to take an attitude interested and detached, not passionately roused but modestly bemused.

After a while, when Hermia and Lysander depart Athens, I

was ready to see them in a romantic wood where love, true love, is all. Transition to the banal did not long threaten. In waking hours we like to know where we are going, and at other Shakespeare plays we usually know. We hear about Belmont before we leave Venice or about Rome while we dawdle in Cleopatra's Alexandria. Dreams provide no such preparation, and neither, in the early minutes, does *A Midsummer Night's Dream*. With no preparation whatever, Theseus' palace gives way to Quince's house in the thumping city.

In 1595 the city meant any of several worlds. At a word, any one of these would spring to life in the theater. Let but an actor say to another, "Your mind is tossing on the ocean. There, where your argosies with portly sail," (*Merchant of Venice*, I, i, 8–9) and the audience followed the airy charm into the city of trade. Or let an actor berate another about sack, benches, and bawds, and his rough magic conjured up a city capable, like pitch, of staining a prince's reputation (*Henry IV, Pt. I*, I, ii, 2–13). The city also meant the world of churches, the world of constables and the watch, the cony-catching world, or the world of streets and market places. In 1595 the city most insistently meant the world of industrious, politically shrewd, ambitious, religious, and frequently wealthy members of craft and merchant companies—citizens. With increasing confidence they were accumulating power and devising strategies that would revolutionize the material life of mankind.

Initially Quince's city friends were recognizable because of their fictional prototypes. To be sure, their purpose to plan an entertainment for great people fit an actual practice of our time. But to every one of us who remembered the Mysteries, *Cambises*, and the degenerated Moralities, who had laughed at John Heywood's interludes or *Gammer Gurton*, Shakespeare's artisans came like a foot to a long-used shoe. More specifically, we readers of Chaucer added Bottom to our old friends, Miller Reeve, Cook, Summoner, and Friar. To their minds tyranny is the great histrionic posture, and love's perils are indelicately blamed on the French.

Shakespeare's artisans, like Chaucer's, produce an abrupt contrast with the scene that precedes: we enter their world directly from lute-song Athens.

Chaucer's trick of juxtaposing Theseus' dukedom and the Canterbury road produces more than the contrast between good and bad, grave and loud, old and new, pretty and ugly, high and low, delicate and crude, though these words touch part of what is accomplished. I doubt that there was ever anything remotely like it before Chaucer. At one moment Palamon and Emelye's tender, all-for-love, impossible world, and at the next moment the sweating fabliau world where the drunken, domineering Miller swears "By armes, and by blood and bones" that he can match the Knight. Bottom swears no such oath. He does not have to. This was 1595, and rivalry, despite families like mine, was obvious between gentlefolk still fostering chivalric fictions and plain-spoken businesslike citizens.

It was profitable to remember Chaucer's marvelous poetic textures. The play opens with stylized blank verse. But in line 167 we heard a phrase echoing the Knight's Tale. It was, says Chaucer's Knight, "in a morwe of May" (line 1034)[12] that Emelye first dazzled Palamon and Arcite, and it was "to doon his observaunce to May" (line 1500) that Arcite went to the wood where Palamon overheard his recitation of love. It was, says Shakespeare's Lysander, "To do observance to a morne of May" that he has gone with Hermia and Helena to the spot where he now proposes to meet Hermia by moonlight. Four lines later, in a passage still recalling Chaucer, Shakespeare's lovers switch to pentameter couplets like those Chaucer invented. The rimes throughout the rest of the scene, some eighty lines, sound the right bittersweet tone for young love adrift in a hostile world.

Chaucer, marking the leap from brave knights and lovely ladies to the Canterbury road, continues to rely on couplets, adequate in his sure hands to give boisterous Host and tough Miller their characters. Quince and Bottom speak downright prose.

Quince's guests abruptly cancel love-sick Helena's implied promise that the next dramatic moment will offer rich romantic pain under the trees and tender us an evening as undemanding as the Reeve's Tale. We doubters further relaxed our defenses against persuasion or involvement. Quince indicates that the wood outside Athens will contain these homespuns as well as the young gentlefolk, yet the play's swift pace hardly gave us time to wonder what embarrassments might befall the lovers when in upon their pastoral dalliance burst these clumsy mechanicals.

Whereas the visit to Quince's house starts with a shock, we accepted in our hearts the flight to fairyland before our minds quite knew why. George Peele's *Old Wives Tale* and before that Chaucer's introduction to the Wife of Bath's Tale had prepared our reflexes. In the 1580s Peele had staged a tale about a damsel red as a rose and white as snow, enchanted most wickedly and then liberated after a rollicking farrago of magic. Peele first paraded before us a clutch of theatrically credible young men who, lost in a wood, find refuge in a cottage. There an old wife begins the narrative that presently materializes into an interlude played by actors while she and two of her guests become a stage audience. In constructing this escape from actuality Peele invites a certain attitude toward the magical world. What is here presented, he seems to say, will not elevate your soul nor illuminate your mind; come share for fun the imaginings of humble folk. Peele periodically returns us to good wife Madge, her one-bedroom home, and her captive stage audience.[13] It is enough if we believe in Madge and believe that she believes the wonders she narrates. We are involved with scheming Sacrapant and vivacious Jack only at a safely condescending distance.

Peele was in debt to Chaucer, who put the fairy tale of the Loathly Lady in the Wife of Bath's mouth. Chaucer makes sure we understand that for all her no-nonsense worldliness the Wife would rather see fairies than friars. We are ready for her tale because we go to it in company with believers—the Wife herself and the even more credulous Friar and Summoner. Tale tellers like the Wife and Madge had commanded our assent when we were children. We knew the land we would revisit during a story from such lips.

The fairyland of Athens in *A Midsummer Night's Dream* does

not, to be sure, come in a narrative told by a wife or anybody else. But it follows Quince's world in a sequence reminiscent of earlier stories. Though Bottom later shows that he does not understand who Titania is, at the outset he and his fellow citizens resembled the fairy-conscious pilgrims to Canterbury, resembled Madge and her husband Clunch. This resemblance influenced the way we first perceived the rude mechanicals, and we who then liked Bottom and his friends were prepared to recognize in the Athenian wood the kind of enchanted countryside that the likes of Alice of Bath and Madge believed in. We were ready to summon up a very particular mood of disbelieving make-believe.

Accordingly, though we had no advance notice of Robin and the First Fairy, they evoked in us and for a moment fitted nicely a developed preconception. Hearing their lilting verse after Bottom's prose was like accepting the music of a familiar dance. Even in the twentieth century you are only a trifle slower when you welcome the fairies to the unpretentious company of your childhood memories.

An altogether courtly group on stage had promptly and effectively defined the first setting, and an altogether artisan group had defined the second. But fairyland drew upon memories from three different realms. It did not long remain simply a transcendent echo of English stories in which our mothers' maids had peopled with sprites our native hills, brooks, standing lakes, and groves. The initial fairy lyric, "Over hill, over dale," though it too bespoke homely memories, was an art song sophisticated enough to lead without strain into preparation for fairy royalty. Oberon summoned memories of fairylands invented for High Medieval romances, and Titania summoned memories of the old Mediterranean world. Shakespeare's fairyland was complex.

IV / The Immodest Demand and a Return to the Actual World

Having perceived the outlines of Oberon's kingdom, I began to pose cosmic questions, and when I did *A Midsummer Night's Dream* responded, teasing that part of my mind which at other times had led me into daring speculations. It spoke to my friends as well as me in the mood of high comedy, tempting us to risk contemplating our own models of the world with hearts as light and minds as free as the hearts and minds we initially brought to bear on Oberon's fairyland. Eventually we recognized that we were being subjected to a less modest demand.

The first step away from playful enchantment looked innocent. Once Oberon and Titania are reconciled, Puck reports the morning lark, whereupon all three, following the night, disappear. Hard upon their departure come Theseus and his hunt, recapturing the wood for a daylight world. Complete conquest is not instantaneous. The belling dogs' "musicall confusion" faintly sustains the moonlight mood, as does the lovers' uncertainty whether they are still dreaming, and so do Bottom's garbled waking words. Although Theseus promises to fulfill the hopes of finally true lovers, the pattern for Jacks and Jills, unfinished, pulls at expectation like an unresolved musical chord. In their second visit to Quince's house, the artisans learn that their "play is preferd." But here too expectation remains poised for fulfillment.

The Athens to which Theseus and the rest eventually return asks to be believed in. The night in the wood had been so outrageous that even the most skeptical of us, half forgetting, felt ourselves returning to a sane environment. Moreover, the canceled hunt, less exotic than hunts in earlier stories about Theseus—by Euripides in *Hippolytus*, Seneca in *Phaedra*, and Chaucer in the Knight's Tale—provided a subtle transition. Though it did not effect a transfer to England (insistence on Crete, Sparta, and Thessaly specifically prevented that), the familiar sequence suggested coming home.

Gone, at the end, is the cruel law, gone and forgotten. The dialogue is again poetic, but less pompous in diction than "our nuptiall hower Draws on apase," less stiff with rhetorical scheming than "Fower daies . . . Fower nights . . . And then the Moone" or "woo'd . . . wonne . . . will wed." Instead of a lyric antiphony over love's delays, Theseus and Hippolyta now dispute amiably, like people in a Platonic dialogue, about proprieties and approaches to truth. The young people exhibit no romantic rebellion, just company manners, like my wife's cousin and his bride, for whose nuptials *A Midsummer Night's Dream* was being performed.

The sense of the actual in Theseus' final Athens took reinforcement from the artisan interlude's very unpersuasiveness. Compared with Pyramus the amused Athenians looked lifelike. Besides, Bottom's audience and we the actual wedding guests were perforce drawn into a tight community: we were all watching "Pyramus and Thisby," and the Athenians on stage were saying aloud the contemptuous things that needed saying.

At first our identity with the Athenian aristocrats felt natural and not particularly significant. The only apparent business at hand was to conclude the evening on a light note and then disperse to bed. Obviously neither Athenians nor we English were invited to feel tragic terror. But the staged criticism of "Pyramus and Thisby" in a sense overdid the modest demand. The Athenians, blatantly and too much protesting the triviality of the interlude, provoked us to feel, "Maybe not so trivial," out of plain perversity. If Demetrius had not quipped that a lion may speak when "many Asses doe" I myself might have made the comment. With the shortened sense of distance from the stage audience, I just a little resented hearing my criticism anticipated. The "malignant and dull delight" is still a delight. As I shall tell you in detail later, I began to feel that the excessively ridiculed world of the mechanicals might be worth thinking about, and I concluded with the mental equivalent of tragic terror in the first magnitude.

After the burgomask dance and the general exodus, we heard Robin briefly conjure up bleak midnight scenes of lion, wolf, and owl, of weary ploughman and woeful wretch, of death and graves. But then he reminded us that we were still in Theseus' "hallowed house," where the small immortals take their stand to banish horror and confer the blessing of "sweete peace." The palace, as we saw, is finally marked by warmth, kindliness, and joy. Over palace and cosmos Oberon is in command. We felt that Robin was addressing us directly in his epilogue:

> If we shadowes have offended,
> Thinke but this (and all is mended)

> That you have but slumbred here,
> While these visions did appeare.
> And this weake and idle theame. . . .

I mused that my Puritan aunt might indeed be offended if she saw a comical god in Oberon, a mercer friend might be offended if he saw all citizens satirized by Bottom, and a few of my philosophic friends might be offended when they saw insipid images of naturalists in Theseus and Lysander and the naturalist world made absurd in "Pyramus and Thisby." But then I reflected that all the mirroring was so funny, not even these sober friends would resent the insubstantial pageant any more than I did, who resented it not at all.

Most of us took Robin's words as a *pro forma* apology, merely the suits of a modest demand. *A Midsummer Night's Dream* had led us by such a route that after this speech delivering us back to the places our bodies occupied, our hands that applauded Robin felt much like hands that were also applauding an actor, very much like the hands that had greeted our host. If coming away from the *Dream* was like being waked, we woke without a start.

Before Shakespeare, perhaps Robin hobnobbed only with humble folk and children. But now he and his master's whole train were clearly the benefactors of Duke Theseus and his guests. To the degree that we accepted community with these Athenian gentlefolk we were ready to join them as recipients of Robin, Oberon, and Titania's whimsical benevolence. Robin made the invitation explicit. "We will make amends, ere long," he said, as if confident that somewhere an hour hence he and his immortal companions would deal with us playgoing mortals again. His offer made the most immodest of all possible demands—that we believe his promise. Nobody in his waking mind refrained from calling "the Puck a Lyer." But when we called him that we laughed.

II · NAMES IN THE STRUCTURE OF THE ATHENIAN WORLD

Make but my name thy love.
—Sonnet 136

LIKE ADAM with the beasts, any playwright must name his main characters.[1] Unlike Adam's, the playwright's labels are potent with old associations, their impact to a degree predictable. In our ears the sound of *Agincourt* or *Flint Castle* vibrated with glory or laid the basis for irony. Those who loved him would have been happy to say that Shakespeare bestowed names with an always sure art. Alas, Falstaff's name, replacing *Oldcastle*, testifies that if Homer never nodded, some of our contemporaries made sure their playwright never nodded in comfort.[2]

For the essential job of tagging characters, *Theseus, Hippolyta, Oberon,* and *Titania* served no better and no worse than if they had been *John, Mary, Tom,* and *Agnes.* Yet *Hippolyta* and the rest fruitfully teased imaginations familiar with the Knight's Tale, *The Faerie Queene, Huon of Bordeaux,* and such classical favorites as Plutarch's *Life of Theseus,* Homer's *Iliad* and *Odyssey,* Ovid's *Metamorphoses* and *Ars Amoris,* and Virgil's *Aeneid.* The names that disturbed our memories led us to build a new and strange Athenian world and encouraged us to sustain a lofty attitude toward the order of nature its operational divinities governed. At length we found ourselves invited to take up a dwelling in the new Athens, to make its people our people, its gods our gods.

Several names in *A Midsummer Night's Dream* have in later times looked like errors stemming from somebody's ignorance or carelessness—Shakespeare's or a printer's—but nearly all the other names are monstrous too. We who first heard them perceived a pattern strange, admirable, and funny. The "mistakes" played subtly with our imaginations, nudging them away from the London of our daylight harassments and encouraging them to participate in constructing a world where we might contemplate with amusement and no anger controversial aspects of thought and behavior.[3]

The construction of names resembled the construction of dreams: known components recombined into new patterns. Poets before Shakespeare had imitated dreams, and prophets had employed their wild metaphors. Waking we hear talk and waking we see birds, but when Chaucer describes a convention of talking birds he describes a dream. Pharaoh's nightmare—lean cattle devouring fat cattle—becomes Joseph's picture of affluence in danger. In *A Midsummer Night's Dream* we found events and situations constructed from parts never before so organized: a peaseblossom playing courtier to an Olympian goddess behaving like a fairy queen who gives to a citizen with an ass's head a welcome fit for Sir Launcelot. Names of most Athenians were dream structures too, strangely derived from familiar components. Some, straight out of familiar stories, belonged to characters marvelously unlike their original owners. English common nouns were names for Athenian workmen and minidivinities. Some names, though they reminded us of characters in stories about Greeks, had slightly different sounds. Two, reminding us of characters to whom Chaucer had given reshaped names, were not in the shapes Chaucer used. Each name reminded us of a familiar way real people with inaccurate memories or disingenuous or poetic purposes have occasionally manipulated names, but I did not remember any play or poem that proceeded with such persistent method.

Though many names reminded us of an admired ancient Athenian world, they did not, taken together, suggest an actual city. In English historical plays using names of known persons doing recorded things in known places, we recognized a tacit claim that "All Is True." *A Midsummer Night's Dream*, only rarely deviating into accuracy, made no such claim.

After a while I thought that names and dreams imitated our new philosophers' modes of designing unprecedented models of natural phenomena out of data already observed in ordinary contexts—but that speculation belongs with later chapters in my story. In this chapter and the next I want to record first the qualities which names conferred upon mortal Athenians and their city, and then the synthesizing power with which names of the immortals helped to create a new cosmic order governing the mortals.

The construction of Athens in the first scene follows a sequence employed again for Quince's house. First a character's name, as if with a quick charcoal stroke, blocks out time, place, governing principles, and mood. Then other factors, including other names, complete the sketch.

II / Half-Remembered Names for a Lofty, Dream-Born Athens

When we who loved Chaucer heard the name *Hippolyta* and saw Hippolyta presented as a betrothed bride, our imaginations carried us swiftly to the Athens of the Knight's Tale. Knowing that though Plutarch mentions Hippolyta, like other ancient authors he usually prefers her alternative name *Antiopa*, and knowing that in Euripides and Seneca her son by Theseus is conspicuously a bastard, we let our less earthy memories confer on the comedy the flavor of early moments in Chaucer's chivalric romance.

The next name, *Philostrate*, also recalled Chaucer's Athens, but confusedly. *Philostrate* appears in no ancient Theseus story. In the Knight's Tale Philostrate is Arcite's alias when, disguised, he ventures close to Emelye in Theseus' court, long after Theseus has married Hippolyta. Although as Philostrate, Arcite becomes Theseus' retainer, he never arranges any revelry, certainly not an entertainment to celebrate Theseus' wedding. His name did not make Shakespeare's Philostrate into Arcite, of course. It tended to confirm Chaucer's Athens, but without precision.

After Philostrate the next character is Theseus himself. His name and rank fit a neo-Chaucerian setting. Egeus calls him "our renowned duke," echoing Chaucer's "duc." Sir Thomas North's Plutarch never uses the title, nor does Arthur Golding's Ovid, nor of course do the Greek and Latin texts. In lordliness he is like Chaucer's Theseus. In the complete reversal of his attitude toward the law he is not.

Hermia's father bears a familiar name, which he deserves only because in Plutarch Egeus is for a moment a threat to his child's life. But in this and all early accounts (including Chaucer's) Egeus has no daughter but a son, named Theseus.

For us the names colored the first scene in *A Midsummer Night's Dream* with an antiquity conjured up (to use the words of Sonnet 106) out of "the chronicle of wasted time" with its "descriptions of the fairest wights." But the cockeyed conjuration kept nostalgia at arm's length.

When Oberon quarrels with Titania he upbraids her for complicity in Theseus' past mistreatment of girls (Theseus was fickle when young—as Demetrius has shown himself to be, as Lysander presently will be—and a Titania not submissive to Oberon's discipline was the cause). The girls' names brought a fleeting suggestion of raw, cruel, pre-Homeric Greece. But the pain was unemphatic, like memories of old, old woes. Oberon does not distrust his recollections:

> Didst not thou lead him through the glimmering night,
> From Perigenia, whom he ravished?
> And make him, with faire Eagles, breake his faith
> With Ariadne, and Antiopa?

Ariadne is a rarity—a classical name undamaged in form and role. In Plutarch and Ovid, Theseus does indeed abandon Ariadne and Antiopa. But in the play *Antiopa* is a blunder. Oberon has forgotten (or does not know, as we knew) that *Antiopa* is another name for the Amazon. He neither distinguishes this Antiopa from Hippolyta nor explains that Theseus has decided to make an honest woman of her. If the reference to Antiopa shows Oberon reproaching his wife for contributing to delinquencies he does not accurately remember, the name *Perigenia* and what he says about the nymph reveal him exaggerating as well as forgetting. Your compassionate editors have sometimes changed the *Perigenia* of the Quarto text to mend Shakespeare's memory or a compositor's eyesight. *Perigenia*, they point out, ought to be *Perigouna*.

It is true that in a summary of the hero's liaisons, North's Plutarch says Theseus took several women "perforce," among them Perigouna. But the extended story, a little later in the *Lives*, has a different emphasis. When Theseus slew Perigouna's father, she hid in a thicket, whence Theseus called her, "and sware by his faith he would use her gently, and do her no hurt, nor displeasure at all. Upon which promise she came out of the bush and lay with him." We held Oberon, not Shakespeare, responsible for putting the more pejorative of two possible constructions on the episode, as well as for forgetting how to pronounce Perigouna's name.

Oberon thinks Titania encouraged Theseus to break faith "with faire Eagles." Plutarch's Theseus never knew anybody named Eagles, but he did have an affair, very brief, with a girl named Aegle, the charmer who alienated his affections from Ariadne.

A passage out of Ovid (bawdily quoted by perhaps too many of us, to make a point exaggerated in your Benjamin Franklin's notorious letter) we took to be the origin of *Hermia*. Like *Perigenia* and *Titania* it sounded just about right to fit a dream of an Athens where *Hermes* and *Hermione* belonged. *Hermes* led nowhere, but in Homer and other writers Hermione is the daughter of experienced Helen and Menelaos, and in Ovid's *Ars Amoris*, *Helena* and *Hermione* occupy a single line (II, 699). The context offers no resemblance to *A Midsummer Night's Dream*, but the words, "*scilicet Hermionen Helenae praeponere posses?*" phrase in a rhetorical question the puzzlement of Shakespeare's Helena over Demetrius. How on earth, she wonders, could you prefer Hermia to Helena?

Helena is twice identified as "Nedar's daughter." We thought *Nedar* sounded something like *Tyndar*. Ovid repeatedly calls Helen (Troy's Helen) "Tyndar's daughter," though Tyndar was not her natural father, only the husband of her mother Leda and conveniently absent when Jupiter waddled up. Like *Hermia*, *Perigenia*, and *Eagles*, *Nedar* played a dreamlike game with our memories.

Of the names to summon up the glory that was Homer's domain, *Helen* has usually been superlatively dependable. Shakespeare's Helena, resisting and at first resistible, is in character nothing like, and in role only confusedly like, the acquiescent, incendiary bane of Troy. According to Plutarch's gentler version, since Theseus wanted Helen for his wife while she was yet too young to be married, he abducted her, intending to wait a decent time for the nuptial. But before long the consequences "filled all the Realm of Attica with wars," and ultimately "forced him to forsake his country, and brought him at length to his end." In 1595 a dramatic world containing a Helena nobody wanted looked very strange. That was before Oberon makes her role abruptly reverse itself to fit Helen's immortal reputation. Then previously unimpressed Lysander suddenly sees in her eyes "Loves stories, written in loves richest booke." And after a while the previously hostile Demetrius gushes a "proper false compare":

> O Helen, goddesse, nymph, perfect divine,
> To what, my love, shall I compare thine eyne!
> Christall is muddy. O, how ripe, in showe,
> Thy lippes, those kissing cherries, tempting growe!

The names *Demetrius* and *Lysander* at one time belonged to formidable warriors in ancient Greece. But in Plutarch these men (Lysander a Spartan of the Spartans, Demetrius a notorious lecher) show little resemblance to Shakespeare's eager swains. The names did recall legendary Greece. They did more, and they did it because they tag young lovers who go puppetlike but with perfect self-confidence into a futile fight to decide which shall have Helena.

Demetrius and *Lysander* sounded crazily like a pair of names from the Knight's Tale—nothing like *Palamon* and *Arcite* but something like the mighty friends who bring armies to a tournament to decide which lover shall have Emelye. Your Chaucer scholars have guessed that "by some misunderstanding" the name of Arcite's "Emetrius, the Kyng of Inde" derived left-handedly from *Demetrius*.[4] They are probably right. Shakespeare's Demetrius resembles Emetrius in that for a while he is belligerent about possession of a lady. Palamon's friend Lygurge no doubt owes his name to the poet's fuzzy-headedness too.

Chaucer misspells the wrong Licurgo, F. N. Robinson records, making him "kyng of Trace" by sheer confusion.[5] *Lysander* resembles Chaucer's *Lygurge* almost as much as *Emetrius* resembles *Demetrius*—mis-rememberings all—and both suggest Chaucer's characters in the same way *Perigenia, Hermia,* and *Nedar* suggest their originals. They reminded me and my friends of Chaucerian heroes as they wage a small war for a beautiful woman. But that was not all.

When we noticed Lysander's name together with Helena's we remembered a love and a war more destructive than Chaucer's. In 1595 *Lysander* (or *Lisander* as the Quarto frequently spells it) recalled the character otherwise known as Paris. Chaucer uses *Paris* and so does Peele in *The Arraignment of Paris.* But Homer generally says *Alexandros,* that is *Alexander,* and George Chapman often uses *Alexander* in his *Iliad,* popular when *A Midsummer Night's Dream* was new. The resemblance of *Lisander* to *Alexander* was more obvious in 1595 than in later centuries. After it appeared in English *Alexander* acquired another form. The great Macedonian Alexander in Chaucer's Monk's Tale is *Alisaundre* and *Alisandre;* and in *Love's Labour's Lost* (V, ii, 567 ff.), Sir Nathaniel and everybody else except the princess calls him *Alisander.* To our ears, then, *Lysander* sounded close enough for caricature to the popular pronunciation *Alisander.*

The names called up memories of Homeric events. When Shakespeare's Lysander, influenced by Robin's eyedrops, suddenly abandons Hermia for Helena, his behavior recalls Homer's Alexander, under Aphrodite's influence, abandoning Oenone for Helen. When Lysander confronts Demetrius, who has the strongest prior claim on Helena, we thought of Alexander, in the third book of the *Iliad,* confronting Menelaos, who has the strongest prior claim on Helen. After enduring taunts that love of woman has made him a coward, Lysander, like Alexander, agrees to a duel. To prevent injuries, Robin Goodfellow hides the combatants with a mist, and to prevent injuries Aphrodite hides Alexander and Menelaos with a mist.

In the *Iliad* two men begin a fight and two armies do fight over a woman, and deities interfere with the outcome. In Chaucer's tale, two men and two bands of knights fight over a woman, and deities interfere with the outcome. In *A Midsummer Night's Dream* a deity interferes before sword touches sword. Memories from Homer and Chaucer, more than half-consciously stirred by the sound of names, provoked my friends and me, in 1595, to regard the hot youths of the Knight's Tale and the *Dream* with a terror diminished eventually into laughter in proportion as the comic world is less momentous than the romantic and the romantic less so than the epic world.

Homer's Alexander and Chaucer's Lygurge are aware that the gods participate in men's affections and actions. Similarities in name and situation point at a notable difference: though Lysander is also completely controlled by the will of a deity, he attributes all phenomena, including his own change of mind, to natural causes.

Individual names and clusters of names that seem to come (but come transformed) from known, traditional Athens thus provided us more than a means of dreaming up a new Athens. We regarded Shakespeare's gentle Athenians not only as lovers. We saw them as comic reflections of men in the actual world (including ourselves) who occasionally have felt lost in the wrong culture.

III / English Names for Athenian Industrialists

When we heard Peter Quince read from his scroll *Bottom, Flute, Starveling, Snout,* and *Snug,* a man sitting near me muttered that Englishmen dominate Athenian industry. Sounding like words in the ordinary vocabulary, the names were more unequivocally English than even surnames like *Howard* or *Percy*. Nobody really supposed that Englishmen had gone to the Aegean before the Trojan War to provide goods and services for Greek heroes. Instead, Quince's house, and with it all Athens, suddenly felt as close to home as a local joke.

Quince, Bottom, and *Flute* were less impressive names than, say, *Carpenter, Weaver,* and *Bellows*. They did not hint at any economic threat or suggest the passionate confrontations that in 1595 sometimes occurred between rich citizen and lord. *A Mid-*

summer Night's Dream goes a less angry way, making high and friendly comedy of a contrast between citizen mentality and courtly mentality. With no bitterness in our hearts we could laugh at modes of understanding trusted by a citizen named *Bottom*, though the more we thought about Bottom the more he dominated our imaginations.

The name *Athens* is repeated again and again in the first two and the last three scenes, but only seldom in the middle of the play. After the fairies announce that they are still near Athens, place names occur as infrequently throughout the long moonlit night as they occur in dreams.

IV / An Almost Authentic Athens

When Theseus and Hippolyta appear in the wood for their morning hunt, Hippolyta speaks of familiar places—Crete, Sparta, and Thessaly. Her recollections seem to shift the scene to a credible Athens near the Mediterranean and on solid earth. But we were familiar with the old stories, and something was wrong at every point. When she tells Theseus about her earlier hunt "with Hercules and Cadmus, once, When in a wood of Creete they bayed the Beare," she confuses facts as if she too were dreaming. The names do fit the heroic age and a hunt is appropriate for an Amazon, but the event is impossible. In the common legends Cadmus died long before Hippolyta was born, and youthful Hippolyta had no opportunity to hunt with Hercules in Crete. Had they hunted, the quarry, as many of your editors have pointed out, should have been a boar, not a bear. However that may be, I heard *Beare*, one more in a series of erroneous details that evoked in comic, dreamlike fashion the flavor of the ancient world. When the lordly Athenians return from the hunt to the palace, they speak without blunder of Thrace and Thebes as well as Athens. We felt invited at last to a believable location in time and space.

Although the first scene of the play sketched a world in many respects more remote from the Athens of Pericles than Homer's Helen is from Aristophanes' Lysistrata, the name of Athens inevitably qualified the romantic world of the Knight's Tale. We never saw technicolor pictures of the Parthenon and had no

Elgin marbles, but we knew historic Athens as well as we knew Venice and associated it with greatly respected qualities, customs, and concepts. Athens was not Rome, but it was Athens.

When André Gide later told Theseus' story, his Athens was big with the shape of Western intellectual objectivity, still barbarous but capable of conceiving a human impersonal justice. Jean Racine's audience saw Theseus' Athens through a neoclassicist's fear: truth and order in Western culture threatened by passion and impulse, even at its fountainhead. Though we lacked Racine and Gide, when we went to a play with *Athens* in the title, we had comparable predispositions. We knew of a city with laws purposefully framed and judiciously, if not happily, administered. In *Timon* Shakespeare later provided an Athens initially responsive to such expectations. If the repeated name *Athens* at the beginning and end of *A Midsummer Night's Dream* keeps poised behind your twentieth-century consciousness the image of the mother city of Western civilization— whatever the play explicitly makes of Athens—you will be responding not much differently from Londoners in 1595. It tickled our self-esteem that after the fantastic fairy scenes we felt at home in the Athenian evening.

We had no wish to eliminate Aphrodite, Ares, Athena, and Zeus from our memories, or to forget that people described by Homer, Virgil, and Ovid seldom behave more wisely than Lysander under Shakespeare's deities. But nothing quite banished from *Athens* the Athens of the great days. Athens prevailingly meant what it meant to Chaucer's Clerk. It meant wit and learning and an attitude toward wit and learning. In *Euphues* Lyly paid Oxford the compliment of loftily berating it, calling it *Athens* and suggesting that the students, "Athenians," were atheistical imitators of ancients like Democritus, Leucippus, and Epicurus.

Shakespeare's Theseus at his worst did not seem a Gothic tyrant. The counsel he gives Hermia, even in the outrageous situation presented by Egeus, breathes the same air of prudent sanity found in the choruses of Euripides and Sophocles. It was this somewhat pretentious affectation of disciplined reason, ascribed to Athens by people of many centuries, which the logic-chopping, rebellious young lovers at the beginning could not abide.

The later Athens of *A Midsummer Night's Dream*, after the irrational events in the spirit-filled wood, somewhat more persuasively suggests the clear-eyed objectivity, good humor, tolerance, harmony, alertness, flexible decorum, and patient recognition of human crudities and follies that we sixteenth-century humanists associated with philosophical Athens. But Oberon is not dead.

III

THE HARMONY AND INSTRUMENTATION OF FAIRYLAND

The nights are wholesome.
—*Hamlet*, I, i

HEN TWO actors tripped lightly onto a stage still thud-
ding with the tread of Quince, Bottom, and their prose-
speaking friends, we knew from the first line, which told us
we were among spirits, that these are not ghosts, devils, or
witches, because they do not frighten.[1] Nor are they angels,
because they do not invite reverence. They must be fairies.
For a brief while, in a condition seldom experienced at a
Shakespeare play, we did not know where on the green earth
we were. England, perhaps? That we were on the earth was
clear enough, for the First Fairy goes on feet, "Over hill, over
dale." Details of the conflict agitating fairyland soon indicate that Robin and we are in the wood where the Athenian
lovers and actors have planned to go.

Joseph Addison in Spectator 419 apparently means to
praise Shakespeare when he decrees that any writer describing a supernatural realm "ought to be very well versed in
legends and fables, antiquated romances, and the traditions
of nurses and old women, that he may fall in with our
natural prejudices, and humour those notions which we
have imbibed in our infancy."[2] Though we learned classical
stories as well as these others in our childhood, Addison
speaks well for us earlier Englishmen. But Shakespeare's
fairies did more than revive early memories; they also teased
at notions we struggled with in our adult years.

The small immortals are not limited by geography or
time. They have connections in India—that vast mystery in
the distant East[3]—and they sound well informed about England. At the beginning they seemed as remote in space and
time as a medieval memory of ancient Athens. But as I went
deeper into the country of the mind where the fairies dwelt,
I became involved in questions that reflected large questions
then vexing London. *A Midsummer Night's Dream* invited
everybody to a temporary escape from the workaday world.
Yet it seemed to speak most directly to us who were ready {27

to perceive old momentous threads warped into a new design, ready to laugh over follies like those in our own world, ready to be beguiled at length into self-inquiries.

Addison attributes to widespread superstition English authors' success in what Dryden calls "the fairy way of writing." But many who responded to stage spirits in the sixteenth century were steeped in naturalist postulates. As playgoers who must learn whatever they learn through actors, we were fortunate that our training enabled us to perceive invisible components of our environment—the forces of nature, the administration of accidents, the intuitions and motives of men—in anthropomorphic guise. Your playwright Eugene O'Neill in *The Emperor Jones* brings "little formless fears" on stage. But such shapes, because they tend to behave like well-drilled abstractions, exercise the passions within a limited if useful range. How can they convey a determined man's power to control events? How can they appall the virtuous? How can they suggest our kinship (or lack of kinship) with the rest of nature, or make demands upon our sympathies? How can they perpetrate blunders, or deceive other characters? How can they dramatize the fearsome lure of human ambition? Or how, by acting upon whimsies, can they comment on our itch to ascribe causes to events which we still have not learned to predict? Shakespeare's apparitions in *A Midsummer Night's Dream* as well as later in *Macbeth* and *The Tempest* did these things in combinations that held mirrors up to moral realities. As provocative as paradoxes in men, they became instruments of our reason.

We acquiesced when fairyland bade us accept impossible adventures, but we sustained our awareness of actual men and the forces that shape actual behavior. We had a fellow feeling for Hermia when, benighted in a wood, she is suddenly, unexpectedly alone. We could see her plight through her own unsuperstitious eyes. Lysander—changing his mind, neglecting his responsibility, coveting another man's mistress, asserting his own virtue, and wanting to fight for his indefensible cause— recalled people we knew. Hermia's bewilderment at Lysander's behavior was familiar too, and Robin's cloud obscuring the moonlight resembled ordinary weather. What we found extraordinary was that for the moment we knew the unknowable: we knew why people and weather were what they were—at least this man, this maid, this cloud. Lysander and Hermia, the wood, the weather, and at length Bottom, Theseus, and all Athens—so we learned—lie within the jurisdiction of fairyland.

We learned a new and merry inflection for our voices when we recognized homely accidents as Robin's pranks, the sparkle of spring flowers as fairies' handiwork. In other circumstances when we saw lovers in trouble we thought of ill-sorted horoscopes, but when we saw that Helena and Bottom were loved quite beside the order of probability and propriety, we perceived there was trouble in fairyland.

The hierarchy of this far-from-perfect fairyland completes the model of a world where love stands a better chance than Lysander's philosophy can allow—a world where seasons of unmerited joy are intelligble. We took a quasicritical stance. We saw that at play's end Lysander's understanding is still one-sided. He has not begun to realize why things happen as they do in his world. We were different. Because we knew why, the knowledge made us wise—wise, alas, only for Lysander's world. We entertained the suspicion that our knowledge of our own actualities might be limited, like Lysander's.

When we met Robin Goodfellow, a fairy king named *Oberon*, and a queen named *Titania*, we felt at home in their new fairyland because we had memories from three different kinds of stories—those kept alive by oral telling, the romances, and the classics. We were unaware of the danger C. S. Lewis describes: "There is . . . a special reason why mythical poetry ought not to attempt novelty in respect of its ingredients. What it does with the ingredients may be as novel as you please. But giants, dragons, paradises, gods, and the like are themselves the expression of certain basic elements in man's spiritual experience. In that sense they are more like words—the words of a language which

II / The Merging of Fairylands Before Shakespeare

speaks the else unspeakable—than they are like the people and places in a novel. To give them radically new characters is not so much original as ungrammatical."⁴

The names *Robin*, *Oberon*, and *Titania*, if we may borrow Lewis' metaphor, announce the employment of a language with three borrowed vocabularies and a syntax based remotely on Olympian Greek. The syntax was not new in 1595, but by the time Descartes died in 1650 many educated people had deliberately relegated it to what they stupidly thought of as a barbarous past. It earned from Dr. Samuel Johnson (who surely had no joyful experiences with dreams, or renounced them when he donned his critical robes) the objurgation that in this fairyland as elsewhere Shakespeare combines diverse and historically incompatible "customs, institutions, and opinions . . . at the expense not only of likelihood but of possibility."⁵

Since you are neither Pepys nor Dr. Johnson, since Newton's world does not utterly dominate your consciousness, the language is no more difficult for you than it was for most of us. Mixed ancestry in the new myth amused us as much as mixed ancestry in the new mortal characters. The Athenian fairyland unfolded before imaginations which, following St. Thomas Aquinas, had for generations reconciled (or confused) several non-Christian theologies.

As far back as Chaucer the Wife of Bath kept two kinds of fairies only dimly distinguished—if at all—in the remarkable mind that preferred fairies to friars. The "dayes of the Kyng Arthour," which she calls up, should be days of romantic fairies. For her tale your scholars have found literary analogues, and her changeable heroine's size remains constant: whatever particular form and complexion she adopts, the fairy lady, as in most romances, is large enough to love a man. But when the Wife wistfully lists the elf-queen and her "joly compaignye, the fayeryes, and the incubus," specifying their habitation in "halles, chambres, kichenes, boures, citees, burghes, castels, hye toures, thropes, bernes, shipnes, dayeryes, every bush, and every tree," she seems to be talking about the folk fairyland. Two hundred years after Chaucer, Madge's *Old Wives Tale* similarly owes debts to both literary romances and folk tales.

The classical element in the fairy mixture also appears as early as Chaucer and as late as Shakespeare's youth. According to Chaucer's Merchant, the "kyng of Fayerye" was Pluto. Reginald Scot remembered what must have been as exciting a household of servants as a child's heart could desire:

Our mothers' maids have so terrified us with an ugly devil having horns on his head, fire in his mouth, and a tail in his breech, eyes like a basin, fangs like a dog, claws like a bear, a skin like a Niger, and a voice roaring like a lion . . . and they have so fraied us with bull beggars, spirits, witches, urchins, elves, hags, fairies, satyrs, Pans, fauns, sylens, Kit-with-the-Canstick, Tritons, centaurs, dwarfs, giants, imps, calcars, conjurors, nymphs, changelings, Incubus, Robin Goodfellow, the spoorne, the Mare, the Man in the Oak, the Hell wain, the Firedrake, the Puckle, Tom Thumb, Hobgoblin, Tom Tumbler, Boneless, and such other bugs, that we are afraid of our own shadows.[6]

Thomas Keightley, who quoted Scot in the mid-nineteenth century, was still irked by the conglomeration. He says: "This appears to us to be rather a display of the author's learning than an actual enumeration of the objects of popular terror; for the maids hardly talked of Satyrs, Pans, etc."[7] But Scot told the truth. The myths had lived in England long enough to enter an oral tradition accessible alike to scholars, domestics, and people like me.

Once free of Ovid's pages, Pan and the rest lost whatever decorum classical storytellers imposed on them. Thomas Nashe in *Terrors of the Night* describes the old immortals cavorting in their new fields of opportunity: "The Robin-good-fellows, elves, fairies, hobgoblins of our latter age, which idolatrous former days and the fantastical world of Greece ycleped Fawns, Satyrs, Dryades, and Hamadryades, did most of their merry pranks in the night. Then ground they malt, and had hempen shirts for their labours, danced in rounds in green meadows, pinched maids in their sleep that swept not their houses clean, and led poor travelers out of their way notoriously."[8] When Fawn changed his name to Robin, Nashe tells us, he changed his habits.

Scot recognized that the immortals sometimes kept their classical names, as when he explains how their misbehaving mortal friends escaped whipping: "After they have delicately banqueted with the devil and the lady of the fairies; and have eaten up a fat ox, and emptied a butt of Malmsey, and a bin of bread at some noble man's house, in the dead of the night, nothing is missed of all this in the morning. For the lady Sibylla, Minerva, or Diana with a golden rod striketh the vessel and the bin, and they are fully replenished again."[9]

Chaucer's readers felt no pain at hearing the folk fairies, the fairy ladies of romance, and Proserpina and Pluto all designated (without qualification) as fairies. We in Shakespeare's audience were more analytical; but informed by the firesides of two centuries, we knew what game to play when dreaming Bottom moves about in a realm that organizes diverse personalities— some as humbly conceived as Peaseblossom and Mustardseed and others with pedigrees in chivalric romances and classical myths.

Dr. Johnson speaks mainly for the eighteenth and nineteenth centuries as he objects to Shakespeare's mixed fairyland. Few supernatural hierarchies have ever been as cleanly definable as Johnson would like. Those that have developed into fairylands have lacked consistency in logic, in the personal morals of their deities, and in their demands on mortals. Sometimes a visit to fairyland brings sensual opportunity, sometimes grim trials of hardihood, sometimes both. One storyteller makes the folk fairyland terrifying, another makes it just boisterous. Fairy ladies in the romance tradition love Sir Launfal and Lord Thomas for no reason at all.[10] Proserpyne and Pluto in the Merchant's Tale influence January and May, but Pluto means to expose an adultery that Proserpyne approves. Even ancient Olympus varies, depending on whether we read Homer or Ovid.

Inconsistent motivation behind forces that govern human affairs? Doesn't that smack of a gloomy wyrd or fate? Not necessarily. We were of Hamlet's persuasion. We could take satisfaction at any moment when we were not being whipped. Though some characters do get hurt in the worlds governed by the Olympians, the fairies of romance, and the folk fairies, some have happy stories. When we saw Shakespeare's Athenians subject to fallible, whimsical, and passionate deities, we were not provoked to unrelieved dread or to any other simple mood.

The fairies' names, sounding in the enchanted night, empaneled on the threshold of recognition unnumbered memories from our childhood listening and youthful reading. A selection of these memories, called up by events on stage, played in harmony and disharmony with them and imparted a rich cargo of qualities to the fairies—somewhat as, deep in an art song, the present music appealed to remembered themes.

The principal fairies come on stage in an interesting sequence. First English Robin Goodfellow, whose name means mischief. His mission, he claims, is laughter. Second, Oberon. Appropriately for a spirit from the romances, he means to decree the forms that define loving behavior and to insure that love, as he understands it, prevails. Titania arrives immediately after him. Her name and her discourse on weather suggest the cosmic forces animating the old Athenian world, the unruly order of the Titans' children. But for all her present wrath, the Olympian hegemony over nature and society appears less formidable when her small person represents it. She kills no Hector. We thus perceived a fairyland dreamed into unity out of three antecedent spirit realms.

Five named characters come from the English fairyland. We remembered Robin Goodfellow from childhood, knowing him also as *the Puck, Hobgoblin,* and *the Lob of Fairies.* But we had never before heard of fairies called *Moth, Peaseblossom, Cobweb,* and *Mustardseed.* As unmistakably English as *Goodfellow,* these names and the sprites who wear them imparted to the Athenian fairyland qualities that modified Robin's.

Robin confesses escapades appropriate to the "shrewde and knavish sprite" whose brittle laughter was sometimes reported in ostentatiously scared village whispers even later than the En-

III / The Component from Merry England

gland of Good Queen Bess.[11] Before Shakespeare, *Goodfellow* often sounded ironically threatening to English ears (especially very young ones) much as *Eumenides*, "the well disposed ones," sounded threatening to the Greeks. Calling furies by a right name was too dangerous. But Reginald Scot and the rest of us outgrew our mothers' maids. When we heard First Fairy identify Robin as "hee,/That frights the maidens of the Villageree" we recognized a bugaboo whose terrors were recorded in old, healed scars on our hearts.

First Fairy soon recalls more innocent pranks and cheerful incidents. Robin reassures the fairy and every audience that, in the rustic spirit Milton would later call jollity he will claim success when a crowd, including the object of his jest, "hould their hippes, and loffe, And waxen in their myrth." No playgoer could retain for this merry wanderer of the night any awe whatever. We could expect—with just enough uncertainty for sauce—that Robin's virtuoso mischief would let us say, "A merrier hower was never wasted."

To Hermia and her friends this Puck's doings will seem like accidents that exasperate poor wights in love. What he does to Bottom's friends will justify his worst reputation. Somewhat later, however, he gives Bottom a most rare vision, fit to be enshrined in a ballad, and busies himself to promote loving behavior among young mortals. He earns the right to be called *Goodfellow* honestly. Yet Robin cannot by himself convey the sweet woodwind timbre of English gaiety. He needs the help of Titania's bright attendants, delicate as their names, docile and obedient (at Titania's behest) even to Bottom.

The attendants' size told us that the new fairyland was not any well-known earlier fairyland. Even Tom Thumb is gigantic compared with Mustardseed. Olympians are Titanic. When a romance says nothing about height, its fairies stand about as tall as mortals. Fireside stories occasionally presented fairies in normal human proportions, but more often described them (as my friends who had seen them still did) in the size of young children.[12] Fairies small enough to hide in acorn cups we recognized as an uncommon breed. Titania's attendants are extremely and contagiously diminutive. Though played by human actors, they and their superiors Oberon, Titania, and Robin all belong to a tiny race. Their stature is not precisely quantifiable, but many details betoken smallness, such as the reference to the "Cradle of the Fairy Queene" and the "little Changeling boy." Puck's darting speed and the mobility of the fairy court suggest hummingbirds more than falcons. Such gods provoke a twinkle, not a Roman thought.

Removal of terror dulled the edge of earnestness, much as minute angels dancing on needle points humanized scholastic awe. Any threat from tiny deities was tiny too. Oberon, Titania, and their retinue won the free-hearted laughter that belongs to the puppet show, to the sylphs of *The Rape of the Lock*, and to Gulliver's Lilliputians. Besides confirming the fairies' size, the names *Moth, Cobweb, Peaseblossom,* and *Mustardseed* suggested the condition of their souls.

Editorial earnestness has given you a strange problem over the name the Quarto spells *Moth*. Some years ago, now, Richard Grant White recorded that in 1595 *moth* was pronounced like *mote*, and said the fairy's name is properly *Mote*.[13] Surely he knew that a luna moth is often lovely enough to suggest Titania's realm! Yet many editors agree with White and with Henry Cuningham who in the Arden edition prints *Mote*, saying, "I see nothing whatever to be gained by retention of the old spelling."[14] I heard the word you spell *Moth*. I shall argue for *Moth* as a pretext for talking about qualities the fairies conferred on the Athenian fairyland—and still confer.

We noticed in the fairy names a reversal of Ovid's practice in *Metamorphoses*. Accounting for the exquisite malevolence of the spider, the beauty of the downward-looking narcissus, the smoothly muscular grace of the laurel, and the idiotic earnestness of the woodpecker, Ovid traces these humble forms to original higher beings. Arachne begins as a girl who weaves pictures in tapestry, and partly for recording the gods' lusty deeds but mainly for pretending to equal Pallas' skill, she ends as a spider; Narcissus begins as a demigod isolated by self-love; Daphne begins as a beauty and ends, because unwilling to accept the consequences of her attractiveness, as a tree; Picus begins as a king whose connubial devotion keeps him from yielding to Circe's charms, and she turns him into a bird unacceptable as husband or lover. The pity of it! We did not need Jaques' gift to suck melancholy out of Ovid's unfortunates. Contrariwise, things which in our England had souls vegetative or at most sensitive appear as divinities in Shakespeare's Athens. Cobweb is typical. He is both Cobweb and a cobweb. Bottom issuing orders to Cobweb is only a step less incongruous than Bottom as Pyramus issuing orders to Wall.

Titania's fairies provoked a laughter recalling untroubled May mornings. Their mortal forms had taught us in childhood to wonder at Nature's delicate skill: instead of the spider the cobweb, jeweled with dew; instead of the narcissus the peaseblossom, fruitful and bright; instead of the laurel the pungent mustardseed, whose promise Jesus praised; and instead of the woodpecker the moth, beautifying the enormous night.

Titania's court, however, has tongs and bones as well as woodwinds and viols. Bottom ignores the delicate images evoked by the fairies' names. He de-etherealizes Cobweb (whom he envisions fouled in honey), Peaseblossom (whom he associates with Mistress Squash), and Mustardseed (who can make eyes water and not for pathos).

Moth rather than *Mote* is the right name for the fairy partly because Bottom says nothing about him. The obvious comment would rub against the grain of Titania's court. She reminded nobody of withered sedge. Bottom promising, if he cuts a finger, to make bold with Cobweb, is funny. Recalling calamities brought by "Gyant-like Ox-beef" on Mustardseed's kin, Bottom is still funny. He remains funny when he mentions an appetite for dried peas in Peaseblossom's presence. Nobody could sigh about putting a cobweb or mustard or peas to their country uses. But what could Bottom have said about a moth that would not recall its fate near a candle? He would have dashed melancholy into the fairy court's bright joy. A mote troubling the eye would have generated as proper a witticism for Bottom as it later did for

Hamlet. Lacking any joke on *Moth*, I was content to associate him with the fluttery beauty you pronounce *moth*.

As the name of Robin Goodfellow brought jocularity to fairyland and the names *Cobweb, Peaseblossom, Mustardseed,* and *Moth* qualified Robin's jests, all of them together said that Titania's court is tiny, not awesome; pretty, not gorgeous; sensitive, not sensual; solicitous, not earnest; kindly, not shrewd; responsive, not grave. The momentousness of this world was comparable to the momentousness of cottage gardens, wherein a great calamity is to cut a finger and a great achievement is to stanch its little bleeding. In such a world we Londoners— forgetting momentarily the hot passions stirred by such cosmic questions as whether a personality capable of being represented by a man born of a woman rules the heavens and the earth— could awake to cheerful wonder, could experience sympathetic pity without sympathetic terror.

We recognized in *A Midsummer Night's Dream* many things to remind us of the fairy romances, especially the situation that later intrigued John Keats—the fairy lady entertaining a wandering knight—and we noticed that the chief fairy's name invoked the romancers' special emphasis on love. We remembered Oberon's name from Lord Berners' translation of *Huon of Bordeaux,* from *the Faerie Queene,* from Robert Greene's *James IV,* and from dramatic entertainments no longer extant. It carried a chivalric rather than a rustic ambience, though in *Huon* Oberon was half the height of a man, like folk fairies.

IV / The Component from Romances

Whilst the table of organization in Shakespeare's fairyland played games with the great Olympian model, the quality of fairyland's cosmic law, embodied in Oberon's personality, recalled elements of the romances—recalled the texture we had learned from the first part of *The Romance of the Rose,* the Knight's Tale, and the milder parts of Edmund Spenser. In Oberon's world love, linked with loyalty and patience, is the ordering force. When he prevails, nature and society function in health.

For minor as well as major dramatic reasons a fairy king served better than a fairy queen. Queenly though sovereignty looked in Elizabeth's England, everybody from the Archbishop of Canterbury to the journeyman over his ale was expected to genuflect before the principle of male authority.

A Midsummer Night's Dream is not explicitly Christian, but in 1595 Christians could tolerate an Oberon.[15] He is a notably responsible spirit. In his extensive biography, *Huon of Bordeaux*, Oberon obeys God, makes stern moral demands on his protégé, and firmly supports the Church. In Shakespeare's play his name served (as Merlin's would not have) to signal his respectability.

Oberon invoked a domestic morality compatible with nesting and with cheerful babies. Where Olympian Jupiter ruled, fidelity was dangerous for men (as Picus learned) and no protection for lovely women. Chaucer's Pluto disapproves certain freedoms, but ineffectually, and most fairy romances deserve their reputation for bold bawdry. The folk fairies often account for irregular human behavior. But Huon's Oberon, more than even Spenser, is serious about family. A celestial king named Oberon can plausibly provide a right world for Hermia and Helena. When Oberon's will prevails, random disorder no longer troubles the Athenian world, no longer roughens the course of true love. Although *A Midsummer Night's Dream* invites laughter at prudery, as when Robin deplores the distance between sleeping Hermia and Lysander, it does not mock virtuous Hermia.

The fairy romances prepared us for qualities in Oberon's queen and for the flavor she brings to fairyland. A fairy lady is apt to be contentious. When she squares off with another nonhuman being, anyone from a giant to a husband, she is as often the victim of enchantment as she is the enchantress. In the intervals between her own affairs a fairy lady quite regularly, like Titania, takes a lively interest in other creatures' amatory adventures, including their marriages.[16] Titania's servitors recall the fairy lady's traditional retinue, and they complement the amorous welcome she extends to her errant knight. They help her to mock the daydreams of any lad who like Malvolio imagines himself surrounded by luxuries and quick servants and adored by a rich and beautiful lady. The unspeakably fortunate guest in *A Midsummer Night's Dream* is Bottom.

Titania's great love scenes with Bottom derive as much of their exquisite comedy from the prior behavior of the mortal women as from romance conventions. Amazonian Hippolyta has capitulated only after war, and Hermia has insisted on the proprieties. Even man-chasing Helena could be stopped by apparent mockery. Nothing, for a while, daunts doting Titania.

Bottom fulfills his romance role in only one respect. When Titania praises his person and virtues, promises things appetizing, beautiful, comfortable, and flattering, makes her servants his servants, and invites him to her bed, he is no more astonished (until he wakes up) than Sir Launfal. In all other respects we found him embodying what was funny in citizen imitators of another stock figure—that is, the true, complete, gentle knight that simplifying imaginations made of good Sir Philip Sidney. To that ideal Bottom's demeanor refers—his modest air, his formal courtesy, his good humor when he makes his wishes known—strangely as these traits sort with an ass's head and a taste for peas, honey, oats, hay, and tongs and bones. His innocent requests played counterpoint to the hot demands earlier fairy hostesses could count on. When not Titania but Bottom purges mortal grossness, we remembered knightly vows. But we also remembered that many city men had teased our minds into musing that their absorption in business deprived them of a loving warmth, a warmth that seemed to us far indeed from grossness.

Bottom's purity as he chooses sleep reminded us of matters philosophical, social, and economic, and we shall deal with these later. But purity, playing against clichés about knights and romantic love, was wedded to the surface comedy. C. S. Lewis has somewhere jested that one cannot talk about decency without being indecent. Turn over the leaf, if you will, while for one long paragraph I talk about decency for those who can stand it. During the test of Bottom's chastity Oberon stands nearby. Despite our awareness that he and Robin had prepared the tableau and despite our conviction that only an addled mind could devise such an inducement to family discipline, we knew the fairy king for an attentive, loving, and demanding husband. We saw in Titania's guest no Midas, no youth panting for erotic adventure but a businessman whose aggressive energies respond to opportunities for a profit. But the ambiguity in Titania herself made the comic situation unique. We had accepted the play's invitation to see a Titania too small to seduce Bottom, while our physical eyes, looking at actors, contradicted that particular impossibility. Our memories told us fairies can do wonders, but the outrageous problem in quantification quite cooled whatever remained of the episode's erotic potential. We watched Titania wind Bottom in her arms and make happy fun of citizens, knights, romance queens, and of all dainty ladies who love the hairy Bottoms of the world, but carnality, the kind that charmed us in *Romeo and Juliet*, peeped out only to fly away in laughter. To all of us except men like Lear, no longer capable of a light heart, Bottom as serious candidate for fleshly lover of Titania was unthinkable.[17]

V / The Component from Olympus

By the time we saw Robin squeeze magic juice into Lysander's eyes we had already recognized the three major components of fairyland—folk, romance, and classical. Seeing at once through the eyes of characters from Athens and through our better-informed eyes, we were constructing in our imaginations a new mythic design to unify the new Athenian world.

Bottom and his friends come close to some of the facts of Athenian cosmic life. When they gather for rehearsal they see at first an ordinary landscape with trees—a green plot and a hawthorn brake—but when Bottom appears with the ass's head his friends recognize that they are haunted. They see the boisterously scary wood we had known as children, whether we heard the proper tales from our mothers' maids or from grandmothers. We saw the haunted wood and we saw more, because we knew in puckish detail what the mechanicals only vaguely guessed at.

When the wood becomes Titania's bower, Bottom does not

recognize her as a fairy lady. But we did. Familiar as we were with romances, Bottom's obtuseness provoked in us an impulse to tell him how to respond to Titania. Our own superiority to Bottom thus beguiled us into playful sympathy with this make-believe fairy queen, and so for the duration of the play we suspended our skeptical defenses against accepting the fairy world.

In the same way our reading in romances made us superior to Bottom, our knowledge of classical stories made us superior to Demetrius, Lysander, Helena, and Hermia, who behave according to familiar amorous and belligerent patterns but (unlike actual ancient and medieval people, and, of course, ourselves) have no inkling that nature, society, and their own individual impulses are governed by spiritual forces. We perceived in their Athens a structure wittily imitating the magnificent myth by which the inventors of Western intellect accounted for the human predicament years before they developed a naturalist philosophy. The name of Titania stirred many memories of that Olympian model.

Scholars in later years who assume that Titania must represent a single prior divinity understandably agree on Diana. After all, erudite King James, distinguishing among varieties of spirits, mentions a kind "which by the Gentiles was called Diana, and her wandering court, and amongst us was called the Phairie." [18] The King tells a truth, but his comment does not tell the whole truth about Titania.

Since *Titania* signifies "Titan's daughter" or "descended from Titans," the name stirred a wealth of memories. All Olympians are progeny of Titans. Proserpyne, goddess of spring, flowers, and fruitfulness and queen of fayerye in Chaucer's Merchant's Tale, is granddaughter to the Titans Saturn and Rhea. Scot's and Nashe's lady sprites with Latin names, Mediterranean goddesses grown old in England without drying up, would answer to *Titania*. The Titan Prometheus by creating life made *Titania* fit any fairy lady whose exploits *The Faerie Queene* records, for all these owe their begetting to an encounter between Elfe and a Fay in the Garden of Adonis. [19] Furthermore, Titania directly recalled Olympus in its heyday. English writers had kept the classics familiar, but it was especially through Ovid and Virgil that we negotiated our debt to the Greek imagination.

Ovid repeatedly alludes to his goddesses' Titan ancestry at moments when they are about to exercise power. He calls Diana *Titania* once, when she is taking the shower bath that Actaeon witnesses at frightful cost.[20] He calls Pyrrha *Titania* when together with Deucalion she ponders Themis' strange prescription for repeopling the earth after the flood (I, 395). Vengeful Latona, Diana's mother, is *Titania* when she comes thirsty to the pool at the borders of Lycia (VI, 346). Circe is *Titania* when, scorned by monogamous Picus, she plans to render him unfit for even one bed (XIV, 382); and she is again *Titania* when she terrifies Macareus with tales of the sea (XIV, 438). However, Titania's normal personality does not merely sum up Olympian goddesses, any more than her enchanted personality merely replicates romance fairy ladies.

She led us to an appreciation of the organic structure of her world, which corresponds (often by reversal and diminution) to the world over which Juno was queen. In both worlds, natural and human components respond to pressures exerted by deities who are themselves loosely controlled by a heavenly society. Orderliness in the Olympian model shows clearest when contrasted with folk worlds animated by sprites more numerous than those Scot lists, each one as independent as Robin Goodfellow before Shakespeare subordinated him to Oberon. Folk worlds and romantic worlds making up the inchoate jumble that Dr. Johnson calls "Gothick" contribute generously to Titania's world, but submit to an intelligible pattern. Where the Puck is, there is forever English mirth. Where Oberon is, there is forever the perhaps mad decorum that English-speaking people traditionally deem appropriate to the formation of homes. Where Titania is, there is forever an unmechanical celestial order fit to account for a dream of an exciting and merry England.

In chain of command and function the new Athenian replicates the old Olympian society. At the top are a king (Oberon, Jupiter) and a queen (Titania, Juno) who sometimes quarrel.

Subordinate deities include a messenger who does the king's bidding (Robin, Mercury). All deities, exerting sporadic influence on weather, flora, fauna, and people, enliven with variety the natural routines.

In the neo-Olympian component we noted modifications more startling than in components derived from folk and literary fairylands. Robin Goodfellow, mischievous before, is still mischievous. Oberon, earnest in *Huon*, is still earnest, and the fairy lady, who in romances enchantingly entertains knights, still enchantingly entertains. Classical myth employed merely for laughter and loving could have been imported equally intact. Instead, Titania inhabits a blithe new world.

The complex quality of this world came playfully to our understandings even when it commented on our philosophies and theologies, because we saw it set in a double contrast. Each aspect of Pyramus and Thisby's godless Babylonian world emphasized a hopeful aspect of the fairy world, and we found that each aspect of the fairy world came lightly to our minds because it reminded us of terror in a nature governed by the arrogant, grimly impulsive Olympians.

The gods in Shakespeare's Athenian world are far from Titanic. Whilst Titania's name proclaims fearful magnitude and power, she is heralded as so diminutive that when she appears on stage her rich anger, unlike Juno's, is funny. Attended always by Cobweb, Peaseblossom, Mustardseed, and Moth, she remained tiny in our imaginations. By the same incantations Oberon, though surely the tallest fairy, looms like a Jupiter only alongside Peaseblossom. From Ovid we remembered Semele's fate. When grateful Jupiter offers to grant any request, Semele asks to see him in the form and power he owns when he approaches Juno in her bedroom. Jupiter protests. Semele insists. Jupiter complies. His presence, brighter than the sun, vaporizes the rash girl. Oberon's presence hurts nobody. Mortals never so much as notice him.

If the old Olympians make man's condition in the world precarious because they are awesomely big and strong, they make it tragic because their deliberate actions, expressing hot passions, so often bring disaster, as Arachne, Daphne, Narcissus, and Picus, as well as Semele, learn. Io learns too. Jove finds her, loves her, and then to keep his spouse from catching him, changes the nymph into a cow. And Callisto learns. After Jove finds, loves, and leaves her, Juno changes her into a bear so unappetizing that her lover lofts her into the sky, a new constellation. Conditions are distressing for a while in the new Athens, but not because of divine malice. Robin's intentional pranks are frightening, but not horrendous, and both Oberon and Titania leave mortals better than they find them.

The Olympian world is peopled with monstrous shapes. Some are divine lovers, less condoling than Bottom thinks lovers should be. Saturn, Neptune, Phoebus, Bacchus, and of course Jove, confronted with a pretty problem, often solve it by adopting animal bodies. With the exception of Jove as swan, they perform the labor of love in menacing form: as bull, ram, hawk, or stallion. Among monsters other than gods, the one most vividly associated with the first Theseus is the Minotaur. Unlike centaurs and satyrs, his head is animal, the rest human. According to the familiar story, once every nine years Athens must send seven young men and seven young women for him to eat. Theseus accompanies the third and final shipment and, befriended by Ariadne, puts an abrupt end to the Minotaur's appetite.[21]

The monster in Titania's world is Bottom. When resting in her arms he is no swan or hawk, no bull or stallion, but a harmless ass. He is not all ass. Like the Minotaur his head is animal and the rest still human, and his tactless words to Mustardseed and Peaseblossom kept us reminded of the Minotaur, emphasizing by contrast Bottom's unfearsome appetites. We laughed lightly over this world where the monster prefers sleep above seduction and for dinner prefers vegetables above a diet of lads and girls.

The old Olympians' jealousy and lust are troublesome enough to individuals. But weather affects multitudes. When the old gods give meaning to natural disasters the meaning is malevolence. At the beginning of the *Metamorphoses* Jove announces that the whole race of mankind has exhausted his patience, though the story suggests that an individual named Lycaon is the burr under his toga. Persuaded to refrain from using his ultimate weapon, he petulantly unleashes the dripping wind. After drowning farmers' crops, the rain keeps on till it destroys all men except Deucalion and his consort. In the foul weather story that Virgil's *Aeneid* tells and Marlowe's *Dido* retells, Jupiter provokes Juno's wrath when, as careless about conjugal fidelity as he is inconsiderate of the boy's welfare, he acquires and refuses to give up young Ganymede. Juno acts from a mixture of motives—prejudiced, vengeful, and murderous. She loves Carthage, fated to be destroyed by Trojan-descended Romans. She despises Ganymede; she remembers Paris (Alexandros), foolish enough to call Venus fairer; and she bitterly notices that both are Trojans, but out of her power. Available Trojans are Aeneas and his fellows. To liquidate them before they can spawn Romans, she pesters Aeolus until he buffets their ships with squalls.[22]

As in Ovid and Virgil, bad temper among deities causes foul weather in Shakespeare's Athens. When the play opens, rains have ruined crops, killed cattle, muddied playing fields, and robbed mortals of their song; diseases abound, and seasons come in a wrong sequence. But not because any mortal has affronted Oberon or Titania, either personally or morally. The logic of causation within this world is the logic in a living body: trouble at one part precipitates trouble elsewhere. Titania says unhappily to Oberon:

> This same progeny of evils,
> Comes from our debate, from our dissention:
> We are their Parents and originall.

The immortals can put a stop to the evils only by ending their own quarrel. In Titania's unhappiness lurks more hope for mortals than the old Greeks and Romans permitted themselves. Her solicitude is comprehensive. She grieves for people as much as for cattle, moon, and roses. She will not discontinue rebellion merely because it causes hardship, but she does miss the joy of the earth.

The episode ensuing from Juno's jealousy over a little boy provided a context we remembered when accounting for the delusions and outrageous actions of the males in Shakespeare's Athens, mortal and immortal. Juno's machinations illustrate the Olympians' propensity to make mad those whom they would destroy. Aeneas remains heroic, but once ashore after the storm, he falls into crazy behavior. His friend Achates says he sees with his mind rather than with his eyes (*Dido*, 326–27).[23] In both Virgil's and Marlowe's versions, deities madden the women more than the men. Cupid at Venus' bidding makes Dido, against her plans and interest, fall helplessly in love with Aeneas. Marlowe adds other unrequited loves, so that eventually Dido's sister Anna is madly in love with Iarbus, who madly loves Dido, who madly loves Aeneas. When Aeneas leaves the country the other three commit suicide, the disastrous domino effect.

Not any god's or goddess' wrath but the same organic world structure that produces bad weather in the new Athens produces midsummer madness in all Athenian men—and no Athenian women. Beginning with Egeus' familial and Theseus' civic tyranny, the men behave unreasonably, but only until Oberon and Titania are reconciled. Our laughter over the merry-go-round of unrequited love, from Hermia to Lysander to Helena to Demetrius to Hermia, stood over against our memory of the tragic straight line in Marlowe. After Titania's reconciliation, we could not know whether her mood of obedience might change again. But while it lasts, Oberon and Titania's concord so orders the world that reason and love among mortals keep company as friendly as twins.[24]

Oberon means to rule, but in the world he rules with Titania the lightnings of old Olympus have sharpened into sparkles. Though no Philip Sidney, Oberon is more civilized than Jupiter. His notions of wifely participation in decisions looked less enlightened than Stefano Guazzo's, but we who were brought up under Richard Mulcaster and such like theorists in education recognized that when Oberon sets out to end Titania's sentimental pampering and make the changeling boy "Knight of his traine," he has purposes more considerate than either Juno or Jupiter exhibits towards Ganymede.

Oberon covets Titania's love. When Titania twits him with Phillida, we remembered Juno's recurring problem with Jupiter's philandering. Juno is right about Jupiter, but Titania hilariously errs. She rails at Oberon for stealing away from fairyland and, in disguise as Corin, "Playing on pipes of corne, and versing love, / To amorous Phillida." To you moderns, even those with more than a little learning, Titania's accusation has sounded unambiguous. *Corin* and *Phillida* name conventional characters in pastoral poetry, and everybody knows what pastoral swains and wenches are forever doing or about to do. But in 1595 we had better information than Titania. The poem that first brought to England the names *Corin* and *Phillida* had often been reprinted since its appearance in Tottell's *Miscellany*.[25] The title summarizes the argument: "Harpelus' complaint of Phillida's love bestowed on Corin, who loved her not, and denied him, that loved her." We remembered that though Phillida is indeed amorous, her Corin is no womanizing Jupiter but a huntsman as impervious to feminine temptation as Joseph or Hippolytus. "Corin he had hawks to lure," and there an end. Titania's accusation provides a glimpse of Oberon behaving as a faithful though not impressively wise husband might behave with a girl who has a crush on him. Juno berates a Jupiter who has committed adulteries, rapes, and worse insults. Titania reproaches an Oberon who has played the flute and quoted poetry. This is the Titania who, eagerly as Phillida, will love a Bottom impervious as Corin! Though we rejoiced in poetic retribution, we did not rejoice vindictively. It is hard to dislike Titania. Her love for Oberon and her midsummer tantrum are compatible with human lovers' long joys as well as their transient agonies.

VI / A Natural
World
Devoid of
Witches

Shakespeare's comic Athens has no counterpart for Hades or Satan or for any of those minions of Satan that King James of Scotland celebrated in his *Daemonologie*. The rhetorical device called paraleipsis enables a speaker to say what he is saying by denying that he will say it. *A Midsummer Night's Dream* denies nothing, but those of us who came expecting witches encountered what felt like a witty reversal of paraleipsis.

In 1595 not a few minds were fascinated by the hating world's dark Majesty and ready to smell him at the first hint of enchantment. Since they detected his brimstone scent whenever they encountered any wielders of supernatural power other than those certified by their own parsons, and since both witch lore and fairy lore had found nourishment in classical myth, it was hard to depict fairies without seeming to deal with witches. Many elements in the play suggested witches as well as fairies: the night, the moonlight, the May eve, the circling dance, references to Diana, the supernatural production of dream states, a man's assumption of an animal shape. A fairy lady was often identified with the chief witch when witches gathered in covens. And Robin Goodfellow's pre-*Dream* behavior was at least mildly devilish.

Spenser praises virtuous fairies, to be sure, making them anti-witch as well as anti-Papist. *A Midsummer Night's Dream* is not so explicit, but a sixteenth-century witch-hunter with any sense of humor, wherever he pursued the teasing evidence that might link Shakespeare's airy spirits to Hell, found his own witch lore itself persuading him to the contrary.

In the very beginning, when Egeus maintains that Lysander has bewitched Hermia with charms and conjurations, the charge is manifestly groundless. Whatever their origins, by 1595 Lysander's love-smitten rituals were only signs in a customary language of adoration and desire. Other witching interpretations were interdicted in more amusing ways.

Whereas witches—as well as Satan when he consorted with witches—were of human or heroic size, the *Dream*'s fairies are small.

Whereas witches had a reputation for bad breath, possibly because of brimstone at home, Bottom attributes bad breath to other causes: "most deare Actors, eate no Onions, nor garlicke, for we are to utter sweete breath."

Whereas witches' hatreds were often held responsible for natural troubles,[26] no malevolence lies behind bad weather in the *Dream*. Although Titania associated the moon with Hecate, the Greek goddess who had grown into an English witch, the Athenian moon influences the floods in the Virgilian and Ovidian way, and Titania's talk about the moon goddess as somebody other than herself absolves her from being Hecate. Further, when at the end Puck uses Hecate's name, it is "triple Hecate," a classical rather than a witching allusion.

Whereas thirteen was the favorite witch number (thirteen to a coven, for example), Oberon, Titania, Puck, and the four named fairies-in-waiting make up to seven. Seven was often a good, sometimes an anti-witch number.[27]

Whereas witches were often females with power, upsetting the right sex order of supremacy,[28] there is no doubt that, though Titania similarly offends, she is basically of the same race and religion as male Oberon, who loves her and eventually prevails. His reign means order, not disorder. St. Paul would approve.

Whereas to get what they wanted those who trafficked in witchcraft had to bargain with and acknowledge the chief witch or devil,[29] people in the *Dream* (with the ambiguous exception of Bottom) get fairy blessings without asking, or even being aware of the bestowers.

Whereas when witches wore or conferred animal shapes, these were generally cat, crow, bear, goat, horse, stag, hare, or bull—Bottom is "translated" into an ass, an animal seldom chosen in witchcraft,[30] and even so his translation is only from the neck up. Bottom's behavior runs counter to the lustful, dangerous, or ominous character of the commonplace witch animal, as it runs counter to the habits of Minotaur and satyr.

Above all, whereas witches were generally blamed for still-births, monstrous births, and at the very least birthmarks, Oberon's fairies guard the bridebeds so that children there conceived may be perfect, without blot.

Some playgoers, humorless and earnest, doubtless continued to think about witches. They saw a baleful Midsummer Night.

My friends and I, prone though we doubtless were to folly, self-righteousness, prejudice, and cruelty, were not irretrievably bigots. We were happy to dismiss witchcraft and give ourselves over to contemplation of other matters. We were willing to speculate about the anatomy of the spirit-influenced world, willing to explore possibilities other than hoary stereotypes. Absorbed in Shakespeare's play, we laughed at the fairies and the pseudo-Athenian mortals and their artificial world. When later reflection brought actual people into the target area of our laughter we did not mainly laugh at superstitious leaders like the King of Scotland, let alone humbler folk. We chose bigger game. We laughed at the limitations and pretensions of people like ourselves. With all our imperfections, we belonged to that fit audience in which you, O reader, find yourself thoroughly at home.

IV PERCEPTIONS OF THE BABYLONIAN WORLD

And trouble deaf heaven with my bootless cries.
—Sonnet 29

T WO WORDS demand rather an apology than a definition. *Babylonian* locates the story of Pyramus as it is told by Ovid and Chaucer. Shakespeare does not use the word, but it balances *Athenian*, and we need it. We are using the word *world* for the total environments of the Athenians and Babylonians because it does not, like *creation, universe,* and *cosmos,* limit us to considering only active principles of organization. *World* can mean simply "whatever is." It implies neither a model dominated by spirits, which we are calling *animist,* nor a model without spirits, which we are calling *naturalist.* It implies neither an intelligible structure nor an absence of structure.

I / The Babylonian World Defined

We who remembered fairy stories, Chaucer, and classic myth understood Shakespeare's Athenian world by understanding Oberon, Titania, Robin Goodfellow, and the four named fairies-in-waiting to Titania. When the woodland rehearsal let us expect a staging of "Pyramus and Thisby" we were prepared to find gods in that play too. We found none—neither Olympians, nor the righteous God to whom Chaucer's Tisbe prayed, nor any other gods.

Following a pattern that could account for mulberries' purple color, Ovid made Thisbe at the end pray to her absent parents and to the gods. The assertion that the gods, answering her prayer, dye the mulberries with young blood hardly suggests a comfortable universe. But it does make the deaths worth something, however trivial and however incongruous with the godless main action.[1]

II / The Babylonian World Depicted by Ovid

Ovid's Babylon contains no dryad, none of the other demidivinities inhabiting Mediterranean trees, rivers, and rocks, nor is the moon called a goddess. Ovid makes no divine anger nor any other intention responsible for the lovers' errors. With the last few lines excised, Ovid's "Pyramus and

Thisbe" proclaims a world lacking the spiritual articulation ordinarily perceptible in classic myth.

Pyramus and Thisbe proceed as if they can depend on their world, but their world has no sense of obligation. They love because they live in contiguous houses, but their fathers say no. The wall joining the houses has a crack big enough for a murmur to go through, but the wall separates as it joins, defeats as it whets desire. The fathers who built the wall expect it to keep the lovers apart, but, flawed in construction, it does not separate them effectively. Ninus' tomb is away from the city, beyond the reach of fathers and easy to locate in the moonlit night. But the lovers' times are out of joint: when they cannot see each other they cannot synchronize their acts. All they arrive at effectively is the tomb.

Ovid's story emphasizes casual disjunctions among the factors of his Babylonian world. Pyramus and Thisbe act on the assumption that the bringers of their joys and fears are conscious of human beings and that events have some moral significance. They express sentimental gratitude to the isolating wall for letting them lay plans to escape. The unanswering wall deserves no thanks. Thisbe assumes that the lioness intends to kill her. She is wrong. The lioness is on her way to a spring for a drink of water. Bloody of jowl, her appearance frightens Thisbe, who flees, dropping her mantle as fatally as Desdemona drops her kerchief. The lioness has no use for the mantle, but nuzzles it, as cats will nuzzle, and stains it with the blood of her recent kill. Pyramus' suicidal remorse is therefore like Thisbe's flight, motivated by a false inference from undeniable facts. The scene as Pyramus perceives it is more false than the handkerchief in Cassio's hand. The bloody mantle is the spoor of a lioness no longer hungry enough to make a meal of Thisbe. It is the very sign of Thisbe's safety, not of her death.

The world in Ovid's basic story exemplifies what Thomas Hardy would later call "crass casualty." Accident leads to accident. It is a world in which "sin" is meaningless and planning foolish.

Retelling Ovid's story two centuries before Shakespeare, Chaucer puts Pyramus and Tisbe in a world comparatively genial. Indifferent to mulberries, he omits the one incident for which Ovid invokes the gods. But whereas Ovid provides nothing for the lovers to care about except each other, in Chaucer's Babylon a fourteenth-century Englishman might feel at ease. Chaucer converts the common wall of the two houses into an outdoor stone wall, separating the properties of two lords who live "upon a grene." Although Tisbe is confined to her home, friendly women keep the lovers informed about each other. Chaucer installs the confessional; he has the lovers "wish to God" and Tisbe pray to "ryghtwis God." He makes even Ninus' burial place less exotic: instead of a tomb Ninus lies in a grave.

This Babylon, with neighborly people and familiar institutions, exhibits modes of expectable response in nature and society. A custom, not a unique despotism, keeps Chaucer's Tisbe at home. Although Chaucer's lioness, like Ovid's, is in search of water, Chaucer makes Tisbe sit at a well, so that his animal has a motive for approaching her. Chaucer fits the quality of Tisbe's world to the tragedy of her decision. Whereas Ovid neither praises nor blames, Chaucer as in other stories that make up *The Legend of Good Women* praises Tisbe for exemplifying a costly fidelity. By giving her the opportunity to choose comfortable safety he makes her a devoted martyr to love.

IV / The
Babylonian
World
Depicted by
Shakespeare's
Craftsmen

Quince's Babylonian world has none of Chaucer's homeliness. It is even more desolate than Ovid's. Notice the weather. In Ovid the decision to leave Babylon occurs on a lovely morning:

> *postera nocturnos Aurora removerat ignes,*
> *solque pruinosas radiis siccaverat herbas.*[2]

Chaucer hardly improves on Ovid as he translates, but he retains a cheery tone:

> Tyl on day, when Phebus gan to cleere—

> Aurora with the stremes of hire hete
> Hadde dryed up the dew of herbes wete—.[3]

Quince provides no morning. The action begins, continues, and ends in "grim lookt night."

But Quince's Babylonian world most conspicuously differs in its absolute godlessness. Although in Ovid the gods serve a perfunctory purpose, they at least exist and know. Quince omits them.

Long before Richard Hooker in the first book of *The Laws of Ecclesiastical Polity* made the assertion eloquent, we knew the doctrine that a world lacking the universal order God's Providence enforces must be hopelessly undependable, in duration brief as lightning in the collied night.[4] The lineaments of such a chaos-bent world, visible in Ovid, are stark in Quince's interlude: each natural thing, obedient to no comprehensive design, follows its own discrete laws and logic. One who tries might perhaps find in Ovid's Babylon, but not in Quince's, an action compatible with an organic universe. What makes Quince's Thisby flee affrighted is not Ovid's faintly dramatic accident of one purpose crossing another. In Ovid the lioness wants water when she comes upon Thisbe; Quince's lion wants nothing at all. In Ovid Thisbe at least holds a conscious dying Pyramus in her arms. Quince's lovers never touch while Pyramus is alive: they begin in isolation, they die in isolation, and only their corpses lie together: their dead world spells no pattern save accidents, no end save death, no hope in death.

Pyramus and Thisby are wrong about the world they live in. Lyly's Endimion speaks no more conversationally to the moon than does Pyramus. "I thanke thee, for thy sunny beams," says Pyramus. And when he asks, "O, wherefore, Nature, didst thou Lyons frame?" he is as unmistakably animist as your William Blake, who, echoing him, apostrophizes the Tyger, "What immortal hand or eye / Dare frame thy fearful symmetry?" Pyramus and Thisby speak less frequently to each other than to Wall, Moon, and Nature, to eyes, tears, sword, and night. They assume, in short, that Nature is responsive to them and that each part of their world has, or is, a spirit capable of understanding.

Pyramus and Thisby do not think they live in a completely friendly world. They do not attribute to Lion, for instance, the disposition of Snug, most sturdily inoffensive of all the kind-spirited troupe. They know nature can hurt them. They do not know why. They endow with meanings a world more remote from actuality than the distance between Helen's beauty and a brow of Egypt.

I cannot report that any of us in the first audiences welcomed the rude mechanicals' model as a world cleared of metaphysical rubbish. But we did recognize evidence of a kind of thinking familiar enough to provoke John Donne, before many years should pass, to deplore it in verse.

The characters in the interlude misunderstand their world so spectacularly that they might have led us to bitter laughter if Bottom and his friends were skillful theatrical producers. But monumentally inept, they present no "Satire keene and criticall." Their dramatic imagination reaches as high as low comedy.

V / The Craftsmen's Staging of Babylon and Babylonians

A world containing ghosts, gods, and other habitually invisible spirits had frequently been put on stage by classical, medieval, and sixteenth-century playwrights. The Oberon-dominated world could therefore fit into a common theatrical tradition. The staging of "Pyramus and Thisby," however, solves a new problem. How may an audience come to recognize an assortment of common natural things for what they are and at the same time see what they look like to a complete animist?

Quince and his players do not know that there is such a problem. They solve it because they recognize a less subtle difficulty. They have manpower aplenty but meager means—though Quince is a carpenter—of setting a stage. One of them suggests that "a casement of the great chamber window" be left open to admit moonshine. However, despite the almanac, a cloud might cover the moon. The accessible stage prop for the moon is a man. The lion, who must not frighten the ladies, had better be a man too. Snout protests, "You can never bring in a wall." You might if you were resourceful enough to produce a masque. For "Pyramus and Thisby" some man or other must present wall.

The artisans' performance is bizarre. Often interrupted, it develops no momentum. The verse is atrocious. Whereas long rolling rhythms can at times hypnotize an audience into accepting impossible propositions, Chaucer knew what Arthur Golding and Thomas Preston innocently demonstrate (along with not-so-innocent John Skelton)—that quick rimes, short periods, and mixed diction can make serious pronoucements sound silly. Nobody ever had worse doggerel lines than Pyramus at the top of his passion.

In Ovid's story, when the lovers address the wall they are employing a rhetorical figure. Chaucer's lovers speak in the inimitable way that provokes one critic to say of their author "naive" and another to say "sophisticated." Quince's lovers lose the distinction between metaphor and falsehood. When Pyramus implores Wall, "Showe mee thy chinke," the actor may represent Snout attentive or ostentatiously aloof as he provides the chink. My first Snout was aloof—but either way, he is still a wall. Pyramus' "Thankes curteous wall," comes from a character who believes an intelligence has heeded his request. The human props are not necessary to the primary tragic statement. Whatever the stagecraft, Pyramus and Thisby would still have lines ascribing responsiveness to unresponsive Lion, Wall, and Moonshine.

Actors representing unhuman things at once provide a ridiculous plausibility for the lovers' animism and strongly emphasize the utter lifelessness of their Babylonian world. We might have perceived the indifference of masonry if we had seen an actual wall on stage. Dead matter's indifference was inescapable when Snout presented Wall. "Jove shield thee," says Pyramus to Wall. But because of Snout Jove is as conspicuously inoperative as stone and lime and, as a force in the world, effectively nonexistent.

VI / The
Babylonian
World as
It Appears
to the
Athenian
Audience

Although as the last long scene of *A Midsummer Night's Dream* begins Theseus finds lunatics, lovers, and poets victims of something deplorable called "imagination," he proceeds to lecture Hippolyta very ably on how to enjoy a play. He invites her to a cool good humor, a quick sympathy with the actors. When he invites her to "take what they mistake" he himself appears ready to exercise sympathetic imagination. But he is not ready.

Bottom and Flute, who act the lovers' parts, knowing that Snout as Wall is a desperate theatrical expedient, invite the Athenians to see an inanimate wall. When Theseus says, "The wall mee thinkes, being sensible, should curse againe," Bottom, who two seconds earlier has been speaking as animist Pyramus, steps lightly out of character and retorts, "No, in truth Sir, he should not."

Theseus and his friends do not perceive behind the artisans' presentation a freshly envisioned, philosophically terrifying tragedy.[5] They are the nonparticipating audience dreaded by every actor, orator, and musician, the barren spectators Hamlet later deplored. Seeing and hearing only a sort of senseless tumbling trick, they cannot respond to the actor's "Believe with me, feel as the character I personate feels," but only to the juggler's "How am I doing?" They scramble together actor and character, device and fictional reality.

They see not a wall representing all the static barriers that frustrate young lovers, but a man who claims he is a wall. They see not a passionate lover cursing all that separates him from his beloved, but a man who can't tell the difference between a man and a wall or the moon. They see not a woman all warm and eager to respond to her lover's desire, the lease of whose love is controlled by premonitory dead material impediments and by her own fears, but a man dressed up as a woman, who talks to another man as if he were a wall.

They see not a lion embodying the unintending and uncoordinated active forces of the world, but a clown who claims to be a lion representing Snug the joiner, who means to call himself Snug the joiner representing a lion. They see not the barren moon, but a man carrying a lantern who says the lantern is the moon and that he is the man in the moon. They do not see a tragedy of imaginative people who ascribe sensitiveness and order to unresponsive chaos.[6] They are not especially unkind, rightly seeing Bottom the actor more conscious of Bottom and Bottom's triumph than of Pyramus' despair. Their failure as audience is a failure not of the heart but of the mind. It is of a piece with their failure, as inhabitants of Athens, to perceive the genial structure of their own world. They do not know Oberon and Titania, the authors of their joys. They see only the palpable actuality before their eyes.

As for us London playgoers, we partly joined the Athenian audience, people like our good personal snobbish friends who sat beside us in the theater, laughing at the same things. This snobbishness shared with the Athenians—and snobbishness may be too strong a word—was compatible with friendliness toward Bottom. But familiar with Ovid and Chaucer, we also perceived the terror lurking behind Bottom's high jinks. We responded to "Pyramus and Thisby" with our hearts as well as our minds, though not even the heart's response was altogether simple. We perceived the artisans creating a world without meaning to do so, perceived that they do not know the world they are creating. For us who relished the accomplishments of London industry, that hurt.

VII / The Babylonian World as a Bugaboo Within the Athenian Dream

As we became aware how terrible is the Babylonian world, our hearts wanted to agree that it is no more than a ridiculous farce. Our minds would not grant full permission.

The Athens we imaginatively sat in to watch the interlude (as contrasted with the Athens the young lovers fled and the enchanted wood to which they fled) felt like an ordered society. We were conscious, as I have said, that this just and loving Athens reflects a loving justice restored in Oberon's small heaven, and we noticed that the contrasting artisan interlude's wooden, unpersuasive fictionality helped to make the final Athens feel lifelike. The contrast worked both ways.

From the vantage point of the gracious, reasonable Athenian society, who could feel that the interlude's world (soulless, undisciplined, mocking men's hopes) holds up any mirror to nature? Is it not a giggling gargoyle, belied by the lovely, winged reality? Seduced into Athenian fellowship with Theseus and the rest, we wanted to join them in laughing Babylon out of countenance with an implicit *argumentum ad hominem*. Who dreamed up this monstrous world? "Gentles"? University wits? No, this nightmare is the creation of amiable blockheads. Nobody could weep over this Thisby, ineptly placed in a false world. How could the story of her plight be any more tragic than an implausible old wives tale? We, however, were doomed to notice reflections of our own serious studies, doomed to find these drawn to sharper focus in our minds, doomed to know that our thoughts were in conflict with one another. We began to lose our share in Theseus' confidence.

Our feeling of proximity to the Athenians relaxed a little when Theseus in his wry way observes that Moonshine and Lion are available for a burial detail; the distance widened a little more when Demetrius suggests that Wall could help, and a little more when Bottom, jumping out of Pyramus' dead character, confirms that like everybody else on stage he has felt no tragedy. A small voice in the back of our minds insisted, "It *is* a tragedy."

Then, just after Theseus and his friends depart happily to bed, the Puck appears and mentions Moonshine and Lion in another way. He recapitulates in a verbal rebus the proper mood of the mechanicals' dreadfully constructed Babylonian world. "Now the hungry Lyons roares," he says, "And the wolfe beholds the Moone." The image recalls Hippolyta's first speech, promising that the moon will "beholde the night / Of our solemnities." To the degree that we supposed her—unlike the native Athenians—capable of crediting the ancient myth, we heard her speak not in metaphor but in fact. The moon, part of the organic world, can wear the name Cynthia and can behold what is on earth.[7] In Babylon, the moon has no eyes. And just now Robin's picture of the silent, static predatory wolf looking up at the dead bright satellite in a moment before he makes his anguished noise brings to Athens an instant of Babylonian desolation more chilling than Warburton's clever emendation "behowls the moon."[8]

The Puck continues his doleful summary:

> Now the wasted brands doe glowe,
> Whilst the scriech-owle, scrieching lowd,
> Puts the wretch, that lyes in woe,
> In remembrance of a shrowde.
> Now it is the time of night,
> That the graves, all gaping wide,
> Every one lets forth his spright,
> In the Churchway paths to glide.

Why so dismal? Why should Robin now revert to his scary ways? For one thing, he sets the immemorial condition of happiness. Keats sang that the right companion for melancholy is "joy, whose hand is ever at his lips, Bidding adieu." Conversely, in this as in Shakespeare's other early comedies joy dwells with encroaching gloom, sadness, and threats of death, but pushes these to arm's length or puts them in process of banishment. Within a few years we were to see Shylock's vengeance made menacing and then thwarted, see Malvolio's mirthless disciplines inflicted and then defeated. Now we glanced back at the bleak Babylonian world which in a few moments we would laugh away from our hearts.

When Robin lugubriously pictures wolf, owl, and gaping graves he gave us in his English audience a sweet nostalgic sense—like that of a child tucked in bed on a winter night in the country, snuggling down the more deliciously because lonely images, suggestive of disasters for the moment prevented, flash across his mind. As when we recalled the Old English parable of the bird flitting through the warm hall, briefly sheltered from the bitter storm, we responded simultaneously to menace and the comfort that "It doesn't touch me. Not now." After Robin's recital of woes, the kind fairies come in and banish the fleeting terrors of the night.

Alas, it is a comical banishment and, for the mind if not the heart, perhaps momentary. Do Egeus' outrageous threat, Demetrius' fickleness, and all the other midsummer madnesses constitute a unique plague, suffered but once, never to be revived? Or are they reflexes of behavior by a Titania now loving but perhaps not fundamentally changed from the rash queen who knows how to slip the leash of Oberon's control?

The real menace we held at a distance was the fascinating naturalist world elaborated for nightmares in "Pyramus and Thisby." Recognizing that this world was compatible with concepts we daily discussed and sometimes provisionally entertained and acted upon, we laughed at the mad play as if it could tickle the funnybone without speaking to the mind. It could not long do so in 1595.

V THE ANIMIST FRAME OF MIND

Tongues in trees, books in the running brooks,
Sermons in stones . . .

—As You Like It, II, i

O Proserpina,
For the flowers now, that frighted thou let'st fall
From Dis's waggon! daffodils,
That come before the swallow dares, and take
The winds of March with beauty.

—The Winter's Tale, IV, iv

T HE MEMORIES of most playgoers at early performances of
A Midsummer Night's Dream contained fairy tales, romances, and Greek and Roman stories. We were all conscious of England's sea routes and of the physical and
spiritual heavens above us. But some of us, from both city
and court, had an additional set of memories and curiosities.
We were full of notions about ancient and modern cosmologies and about the dangers besetting superstitious and
atheistical ways of thinking. We were eager to know well
and truly the structure of our world. Competing world
models and meditations on natural philosophy that might
give us control over nature (if I may exaggerate) were as
magnetic to our attention as thoughts of love. We believed
that world models influence actions as well as thoughts.

We had at our disposal two frames of mind, the animist
and the naturalist; and logically incompatible though we
knew they were, we used both frames with very little em-
barrassment. By "frame of mind" I mean a recognizable
mode of thought together with the assumptions, questions,
and attitudes toward phenomena that usually accompanied
the mode.

Not every twentieth-century commentator has agreed
that cosmology, invention, and business affairs had much to
do with the original impact of *A Midsummer Night's
Dream*. Marjorie Nicolson in *The Breaking of the Circle* describes Englishmen's study of cosmology and with justice
says of Shakespeare, "He was much more interested in man
than in the universe."[1] Yet we who thought he wrote for us
were interested in the universe, and we responded to dramatic representations of differing worlds. When Elizabeth
Drury died a few years later, my friend John Donne grieved
that she died in a world now, so the new philosophy taught,
also dead.[2] In 1595 Donne already understood the old and
the new.

In our animist frame of mind we all prayed, and for the purposes enumerated in Shakespeare's Sonnet 14 many had recourse to astrology. Practical men were driving England into her intellectual, industrial, imperial future, and souls like me valued naturalist experimentation for promising new devices profitable in manufacture. We welcomed a reliably quantified, mapped heaven for swift shipment of cargo. In an animist frame of mind we could blame Robin Goodfellow when a churnful of milk failed to make butter, and in a naturalist frame of mind we could inquire into temperature and the cream content of the milk.

Though struggling to be rid of veils that concealed the body of nature, we had not succumbed to the uncomplicated naturalist frame of mind that scientists from the seventeenth to the early twentieth century tried to bestow on bookish people in the Western World. We sometimes recognized alternatives. We remembered Plato objecting to myth, Scot and Nashe poking fun at witch lore, and Marlowe occasionally talking like the fool who hath said in his heart there is no God. We were prepared to have a partially objective appreciation of our own animist frame of mind while we laughed at Pyramus as Bottom plays him— and we were equally prepared to have a wary appreciation of our own naturalist frame of mind while we laughed at Lysander carefully explaining the natural reasons why he had just left Hermia for Helena.

II / Mortal Pyramus and Natural Philosophers

You would falsify the sixteenth century if you should see Pyramus reflecting only "the unskillful." The ancient models retained power even over leading naturalist philosophers who advocated direct observation and experiment. Nicolaus Copernicus, William Gilbert, and Johannes Kepler were part of the context for Pyramus, the complete, indomitable animist. Playgoers were not more modern than these great wits. If Pyramus' chat with Wall did not look absolutely different from pronouncements by admired natural philosophers, we could comfortably include ourselves, or part of ourselves, as targets of our merry laughter.

We remembered Copernicus waxing eloquent over his model of the planetary system. Thomas Digges translates his Latin:

In the midst of all is the Sun.

For in so stately a temple as this who would desire to set his lamp in any other better or more convenient place than this, from whence uniformly it might distribute light to all, for not unfitly it is of some called the lamp or light of the world, of others the mind, of others the Ruler of the world. . . .

Trismegistus calleth him the visible god. Thus doth the Sun like a king sitting in his throne govern his courts of inferior powers.[3]

Copernicus was not merely indulging a fanciful simile. He saw more in common between the sun and a consciously governing personality than a sonneteer saw between his mistress' breasts and snow. Digges refrains from presenting Copernicus at his most animist moment, for as he translates he omits "*Concipit interea a Sole terra et impraegnatur annuo partu*,"[4] which he might have rendered, "The earth, conceiving by the sun, gets pregnant every year."

Later evangelistic naturalists made Copernicus their leader in the great revolt from awe and so wagged him in the face of ecclesiastics that these came to regard him as a foe to Christian faith. But he did not so regard himself, and for years the developing Copernican model did not clash with our animist habits of understanding. For want of an uproar, some historians, like George T. Buckley, have thought that "general writers and the population at large seem to have been unconscious of or not much interested in the era-making discoveries of . . . Copernicus."[5] We were very much interested, but we were not outraged. To the frame of mind that Bottom's Pyramus comically mirrors, Copernicus felt congenial. We continued to find in the planetary system a chapter of the book of Nature, evidence of a knowing, caring, and patterning Providence. We could look at the solar system, recite "The heavens declare the glory of God," and cast a horoscope.

Congenial also were later astronomers as they charted the bright patins coursing across heaven, a sky determining and responding to that newly important and always mysterious thing called time. They remained tolerable when they warned that what seems motionless might be in motion, that even motion and motionlessness are not simple, that planets are not the only wanderers in heaven and even "constant as the northern star" contains an irony. They still depicted a heaven making general promises it would fulfill in detail, promises to navigators as well as to people anxious about personal destinies. The postulate of cosmic order is very beautiful; it is compatible with belief in a still active Creator, and as an approach to understanding man's relationship to the world it is older than Ptolemy. When Thomas Digges, improving on Copernicus, mapped a universe where the stars did not lodge upon a perfect sphere but were scattered to infinity,[6] his model still gave answers when men asked the practical questions that arose within the animist frame of mind.

William Gilbert was at work on his great book when we first laughed at Pyramus. Gilbert was a dedicated Copernican respected by Galileo and Kepler, subsidized by Queen Elizabeth, belittled by Francis Bacon, later praised by Henry Hallam as "the father of experimental philosophy,"[7] and esteemed by Thomas Henry Huxley as a more authentic scientist than Bacon.[8] Gilbert insists upon his mathematical credentials. But in a whole chapter of *De Magnete*, published in 1600, he develops an argument that "the magnetic force is animate, or imitates a soul; in many respects it surpasses the human soul while that is united to an organic body." He cites Thales, who "declares the loadstone to be animate, a part of the animate mother earth and her beloved offspring."[9] Maybe you can tolerate lyricism in a natural philosopher, but for Gilbert as for Pyramus and Copernicus metaphor disappears into assertion. Listen to his elevated prose:

As for us, we deem the whole world animate, and all globes, all stars, and this glorious earth, too, we hold to be from the beginning by their own destinate souls governed and from them also to have the impulse of self-preservation. . . . If there is aught of which man may boast, that of a surety is soul; even God, by whose rod all things are governed, is soul. . . . Pitiable is the state of the stars, abject the lot of earth, if this high dignity of soul is denied them, while it is granted to the worm, the ant, the roach, to plants and morels; for in that case worms, roaches, moths, were more beauteous objects in nature and more perfect, inasmuch as nothing is excellent, nor precious, nor eminent, that hath not soul.[10]

Gilbert made his magnet spherical, not to exert a stronger pull—he knew it did not—but to have the same shape as the earth, which he found is one huge magnet. Things that behave alike obviously have like souls, and nature had shown that the right shape to embody the soul of a magnet is a sphere. Bottom's Pyramus saying "Thankes" to a wall thinks he lives in the kind of world where a piece of iron ore has a soul.

Johannes Kepler is another distinguished instance of the still complex mind that inhabited men admired now by scientists. Through him you can get an inkling of how animistic thought was giving birth (all unwillingly) to naturalist concepts. Because of Kepler's elliptical planetary model, accounting for Tycho Brahe's data, post-Newtonian men have thought of orbiting spheres without seeing in them an object lesson in God's perfect creation. Not Kepler.

In addition to Marjorie Nicolson's *Breaking of the Circle*, two essays—Wolfgang Pauli's contribution to Carl J. Jung's *The Interpretation of Nature and the Psyche* and Arthur Koestler's *The Watershed*—explore the ties that bound Kepler to astrology, witchcraft, and mystical philosophy. Pauli notes that "in Kepler's view the planets are still living entities, endowed with individual souls,"[11] and Koestler succinctly records Kepler's belief that God created the sphere and the solar system after his own trinitarian image: center and sun after God the Father, surface and planets after God the Son, intervening connections after God the Holy Ghost.[12] The concept so animated Kepler in his mathematical labors that he can sound like Gilbert—or like Bottom's Pyramus: "Finally, those motive powers of the stars share in some way in the capacity of thought so that as it were they understand, imagine, and aim at their path, not of course by means of ratiocination like us human beings but by an innate impulse implanted in them from the beginning of Creation; just so do the animal faculties of natural things acquire, though without ratiocination, some knowledge of their goal to which they direct all their actions." [13]

Though at critical moments Copernicus and Kepler may have banished from their minds everything but the necessities of accumulated data, they did not entirely abjure the comfort of ancient animistic authority. Both echoed Pliny, who in Holland's English translation says: "Believe we ought, this sun to be the very life, and (to speak more plainly) the soul of the whole world, yes, and the principal governance of nature: and no less than a God or divine power, considering his works and operations." [14]

When you remember Copernicus, Gilbert, and Kepler and reflect that we Englishmen in Shakespeare's first audience were as apt as these mighty minds to ascribe sensible souls to things like the sun, the earth, and the loadstone, the one-sided conversation with the wall conducted by Bottom's Pyramus may seem to sound like normal sixteenth-century citizens' discourse. But of course it does not. My friends among London craftsmen, financiers, and merchants, traditional as their speech remained in prayer and in matters of morals and cosmology, were not content with an animist understanding of matters that could be put to experimental test. They often looked at masonry, weaving, and navigation with naturalist eyes and handled mortar, looms, and ships in the naturalist way. But they knew and did not despise the verbal doctrine of souls.

Theseus, Lysander, and the rest of Shakespeare's Athenians ridicule in Pyramus' world an extreme animist model with which they have no sympathy. But active minds in our audience, when we contemplated Pyramus talking to Wall and Moonshine, were apt to laugh a trace more thoughtfully, remembering Copernicus' bossy sun, Gilbert's soulful magnet, and Kepler's homiletic solar system.

III /
Shakespeare's
Fairies and
Questions
of Daily
Living

Though my friends and I found Pyramus funny, we had no thought of utterly renouncing the animist frame of mind. The organic structure of Oberon's world spoke to us in a language we understood. Animist minds tended to put things together, sometimes in strange physical ways—as in satyr, Pan, Minotaur, and centaur—sometimes in models for understanding, as that man is part beast and part angel. We felt no strain at seeing three kinds of immortals in one hierarchy. This urgency for harmony among forces and things superficially different entered into our relationships, our joys, our obligations, and our awareness of our place in society and in the great world.

Within the animist frame gentle as well as humble people continued to perceive our personal identities (as witness our Providential view of history) and our sense of moral and social obligation (as witness the marriage ritual, oaths of allegiance, oaths of office, and oaths in court testimony).

In our animist moments we laid a greater emphasis upon enjoying than upon mastering nature, responding with friendly delight to the sound of a vowel or an oboe, to a piece of marble or monumental alabaster, or to the earth's prolific dust in forest or cultivated field. Our sense of kinship with an organic world was poetic. We remembered and cherished sympathies learned from less skeptical people—from old wives, from classical mythmakers, from the Psalms and Jesus' parables, and from old poets and poetic spirits in the Christian tradition. We knew well how to make believe, when making believe was for joy. As Oberon's artificial world held up a comic mirror to the concept of a world organism, we felt at ease. It spoke to us about questions current in our London, some modest, some that stretched our minds.

When Athenian mortals speak in animist metaphors, the most determined atheists in our midst—so much earlier than Alain Robbe-Grillet—were equipped to understand and not resent them. When, for example, we heard Theseus speak of the moon sponsoring women's virginity, we did not call him a Pyramus. Rather, memories of old proverbs, stories, and customs clustering about words for the moon gave us a livelier context than you usually feel when you speak of the lunatic fringe. A man who scoffed at fairy toys as contemptuously as Theseus might still avoid sleeping in direct moonlight, repeating as a jest that the variable planet might addle his pate. Or he might prefer to woo his sweetheart under Cynthia's enchantment rather than under the all-disclosing sun. To men who had danced and spoken the playful rituals of dread and hope, animist metaphors summoned up gamesome kinetic and verbal echoes. In comedy these appealed more to the wit than to the heart, but they appealed to a wit that remembered the heart's trepidations.

When an aesthetic experience demanded a phrase, we were again apt to reaffirm our fellowship with the natural world. We answered Tamburlaine's unanswerable "What is beauty? saith my suffering, then," with the classic Athenian evasion that beauty is Aphrodite's and Persephone's doing. We could manage verbs in a naturalist context, of course. When Theseus said, "Take time," or Lysander said, "O take the sense, sweete, of my innocence," we took each "take" as simply as Robert Boyle did when he said, "Take two ounces." But we were prepared for Perdita's generous verb when she would speak of "daffodils / That . . . take / The winds of March with beauty." Depending on what the story tells, one who takes may surprise, enchant, delight, or merely receive; a bridegroom takes his bride, a lover his mistress, a pursuer his quarry. From the vestiges of these and unnumbered human and supernatural contexts, Perdita's "take" builds its multiple meaning—out of events which living creatures have performed and we remember.

At *A Midsummer Night's Dream* we were happy to take for granted men's cousinship with flowers when First Fairy announces his chore:

> I must goe seeke some dew droppes here,
> And hang a pearle in every couslippes eare.

We also liked to echo the Hebrew who prayed, "Let the beauty of the Lord our God be upon us." We could construe in the syntax of both animist traditions what Wordsworth in *The Prelude* was to call "The ghostly language of the ancient earth."

Shakespeare's Athenians use a language with Olympian cadences, but the accents of their own animated world they have never heard. Intimations of nature's abundance, teasing them to an awareness of her great creating beauty without showing her full form, come at moments of comic wonder to high and low characters—and their bemusement stands in contrast with the confidence of Christians who looking about on a green and lovely England remembered that God made it and called it good. When he wakes from enchanted sleep, Demetrius speaks for the gentle lovers, acknowledging vistas he has glimpsed but not comprehended, "Like farre off mountaines turned into clouds." A divine bounty has touched them, and they cannot account for it. When Bottom recalls his enchanted experience with Titania, speaking for mortal fools who have put on a demeanor of mastery in situations beautiful beyond tears, he botches Scripture: "The eye of man hath not heard, the eare of man hath not seene, mans hand is not able to taste, his tongue to conceive, nor his hearte to report, what my dreame was." The Athenians do not know—as we in Shakespeare's audience knew—how to behold the untoiling lilies of the field.

When the Athenians fall into ordinary miseries, we were prepared to recognize comic alternatives to religious consolations. The grave Christian met the clumsiness and frustrations of old bones with a faith preferring spiritual grace to agility and power. Oberon's gentle Athenians know no spiritual recourse, but we speculated that when the awkwardnesses of age should overtake them it would be well for them to know about Robin, who sometimes dribbles ale down an old woman's dewlap. They could believe that he is up to characteristic pranks and laugh, ruefully sweetening disgust by blaming Puck. God's own presence accompanied the lonely Christian. In Oberon's Athens ridiculously abandoned Bottom is entertained by Titania. The Christian countered outward dangers and inward guilt in metaphors of shepherd and redeemer. Oberon's Athenians do not know what preserves them. They do not know that Robin protects Demetrius from Lysander and Lysander from Demetrius. They do not know why the follies of both are followed not by exile, murder, and loss of lovely women but by delight. We knew about Oberon. We recognized in Oberon's animate world an invitation to the consolations of laughter.

IV / Oberon's
Rule and
Questions of
a Healthy
Natural
Order,
Justice,
and Loving
Tolerance

Though Pyramus addressing Wall sounds like Gilbert and Kepler, whose animist moments embarrass your twentieth-century historians of science, his question, "Wherefore, Nature, didst thou Lyons frame?" puts him in the company of more moderate men who, while they did not proclaim souls in iron artifacts and planets, still ascribed consciousness, will, and purpose to Nature. Among these less-raw animists, Dr. William Harvey in his *Anatomical Disquisition on the Motion of the Heart and Blood in Animals* asserts, "Thus nature, ever perfect and divine, doing nothing in vain, has neither given a heart where it was not required, nor produced it before its office had become necessary."[15] Confirming Aristotle on the sovereignty of the heart, he notes that it is formed before the rest of the body and that thereafter "nature willed that it should . :. fashion, nourish, preserve, complete the entire animal, as its work and dwelling place: the heart, like the prince in a kingdom, in whose hands lie the chief and highest authority, rules over all; it is the original and foundation from which all power is derived, on which all power depends in the animal body."[16]

This constantly repeated simile of an intelligent ruler in society lies behind Bacon's phrasing of the classic argument from design, behind his view of a world where all individual things, animate and inanimate, are organically interconnected, observing, as Richard Hooker had said, a law "which toucheth them as they are sociable parts united into one body."[17]

Though we had already encountered even in the theater the experience of looking critically at traditional modes of thought —nobody who has felt the fearful impact of Marlowe's *Doctor Faustus* can doubt it—we still habitually tested a proposed action by assessing its fit into God's purposes. In geometry we might feel at ease with another axiom, but when we talked about complex but intelligible events in Nature or in any part of Nature, we tended to start from the model of a governing mind.

We were familiar with large questions which comprehended the mystery of forgiveness and the fear of damnation. The divine mind—so ran one of the gentler answers—forever knows the proper forms of events. That mind anciently granted man power of choice and thus sadly permitted troubles under the moon. But because it continually nudges events back toward conformity with the great kinetic design which it remembers, an evil sequence following a sin or other calamity does not make conditions permanently more wretched but runs its course and ends. In Athens, whether committed by mortals or by immortals (including Oberon himself), error similarly if less gravely runs its course. Oberon, who has a reasonably good if not perfect memory for how things have been, can and does move to put the Athenian cosmos back in order, and he also sets about rectifying specific errors made by Robin Goodfellow, Lysander, and Demetrius. When the Athenian world goes right, Oberon, Titania, and their retinue can fruitfully pursue activities that make the end of love, whimsical though love may be, not death but life. The Athenian world happily imitates the whole orthodoxy which, commonplace in 1595, has been described for you in the twentieth century by such able scholars as Hardin Craig, Theodore Spencer, E. M. W. Tillyard, and more recently S. K. Heninger.[18] Oberon's persistence (until Titania can no longer stomach Bottom, and Athens is freed from the side effects of her disordered affection) exemplifies cosmic memory and purpose benevolently operating—comically because Titania wooing Bottom looks not so much like a step toward a healthy order as like confusion worse confounded, and because miniature Oberon is such a bungling incarnation of divine mind.

Hooker describes the basis for hope under a deity more reliable than Oberon: "No certain end could ever be attained, unless the actions whereby it is attained were regular; that is to say, made suitable, fit, and correspondent to their end, by some canon, rule, or law. Which thing doth first take place in the works even of God himself."[19] The order of nature depends explicitly on "the settled stability of divine understanding."[20]

To those who agreed with Hooker's principle and to many

who were willing to wonder, the only alternative appeared to be a rapidly disintegrating world. In a pronouncement that recalled Ovid's account of the Flood and provided a recent context for Titania's weather report, Hooker elaborates:

Now if nature should intermit her course, and leave altogether though it were but for a while the observation of her own laws; if those principal and mother elements of the world, whereof all things in this lower world are made, should lose the qualities which now they have; if the frame of that heavenly arch erected over our heads should loosen and dissolve itself; if celestial spheres should forget their wonted motions, and by irregular volubility turn themselves any way as it might happen; if the prince of the lights of heaven, which now as a giant doth run his unwearied course, should as it were through a languishing faintness begin to stand and to rest himself; if the moon should wander from her beaten way, the times and seasons of the year blend themselves by disordered and confused mixture, the winds breathe out their last gasp, the clouds yield no rain, the earth be defeated of heavenly influence, the fruits of the earth pine away as children at the withered breasts of their mother no longer able to yield them relief: what would become of man himself, whom these things now do all serve? See we not plainly that obedience of creatures unto the law of nature is the stay of the whole world? [21]

To paraphrase Dionysius, the sole imaginable world lacking God's intellectual control was a machine, able to continue functioning only if perfect. Without a governing mind, the world machine once touched by any irregularity, accident, or shock that might put it ever so slightly out of frame, would warp more and more, strain compounding strain, until it went to pieces. [22]

The animist model accounts for the way things go wrong as well as the way they are righted. For example, when Oberon operates directly upon an Athenian, he is not thwarted, but when Athens is out of frame and he commits an action to Robin as deputy, he commits it to that most fallible of human miracles, communication. Robin may be just as willing to obey as the winged god Mercury, despite his mischievous nature, but he illustrates the incapability of language to convey all of one mind's intent into another mind. Lysander, sleeping at a reluctant distance from Hermia, fits Oberon's description of Demetrius—a disdainful youth in Athenian garments. Robin's role, humanizing celestial error, makes the Athenian deities more forgivable than inexorable, makes determinism for mortals in Athens so faulty and remediable that it apes free will.

To the animist part of our souls the question what, if anything, an event or life signifies was apt to have an affirmative answer rather than Macbeth's despairing negative. Oberon's world lured us along a familiar road. Trained to look for appropriate relationships between any event and larger and larger contexts until the event showed its place in the divine mind, we were ready to deal with Lysander's sudden preference for Helena above Hermia. We understood it as one of the Athenian world's disturbed reactions to the trouble Titania has wrought.

Mustering so great a system to understand Lysander's fickleness is using a cannon to kill a fly. This part of the comedy touched home because the process corresponded to a routine mode of explanation. We noted that woes and joys in Athens give evidence of turmoil and tranquillity between Oberon and Titania in the same way that we ascribed trials and blessings in our actual lives to Providence. Acquainted at first or second hand with Augustine and Aquinas, More and Erasmus, Copernicus and Ptolemy, Recorde and Digges, Calvin and Hooker, we well understood equations between the attributes of God and specific formulations of human and natural events.

Questions of meaning were closely bound up with questions of divine and human justice. A vivid *Abridgement of the Institution of Christian Religion*, 1587, converts Calvin's thought into a dialogue "wherein brief and sound answers to the objections of the adversaries are set down." The "objections" speak fairly well for secular, sometimes naturalist positions. The strain on the protagonist peeps out when he is called on to tell what God did before the creation. He first recalls the answer of a pious old man, "He made Hell . . . for curious men," and then proceeds with a more sober exposition.[23]

This was the fascinating Hell from which new philosophers, like Calvin in their queries if not their answers, were diligently exploring the moral as well as the natural world. In secular moments we debated naturalist questions of pain, pleasure, prudence, virtue, and determinism, and in our Christian moments we debated questions of God's will, questions of faith, good works, sin, damnation, and salvation. For questions resembling these mighty ones Oberon's world affords tidy little answers, comically provocative when one notices that, with a logic like the logic in sober Christian theology, they ensue from Oberon's knowledge and power, his likes and dislikes, his posture toward mortal men and the responsive relationships among the parts of his world. Despite naturalist propensities, we were ready to contemplate problems of justice—what ought to happen to people and what ought they to do—as problems in divinity. We were willing to explore them dissociated from agony, in comic miniature, in *A Midsummer Night's Dream*.

Thinkers about God's justice have from time immemorial felt a tension between emphasis upon measurement, the great symbol being a set of balances, and emphasis upon a divine personality who likes to give gifts. Some thinkers, devoted to the blindfolded Roman goddess and dominated by Roman ideas of order, stressed laws. They searched out God's habits and began to lay the basis for a world not from moment to moment governed by discriminating mind or passionate spirit but obedient to statutes obviously enacted at the beginning of time. The emphasis was older than the first Psalm, but by the end of the sixteenth century it had taken peculiar courses. We were concerning ourselves with numerical precision, as when Robert Greene castigated cheating colliers who used smaller than standard bags,[24] Deloney celebrated the story that Henry I standardized the cloth yard for all England,[25] and on the continent Tycho spent his life using numbers to track the planets. Many of us developed a faith in verbal accuracy, as when the courts, out-Shylocking Shylock and Portia, pretended that one could tell the whole truth and nothing but the truth. To satisfy a moral equation some still supposed that the miserable on earth had been wicked and the happy good. Others, in a measurement grimmer than Hamlet's, asserted that all deserve damnation, and that except for a few miraculously exempt, every soul must endure (besides earthly plagues, earthquakes, unjust judges, malicious neighbors, and unkind relatives) down to the last spiritual dram, a compensating agony in the everlasting bonfire. Wherever men emphasized a world view implying government according to a quantifiable, retributive justice, the image of an interested, attentive God grew dim.

A statutory justice, inflexible as algebra, marks Theseus' Athens at the beginning when Oberon is worried by Titania's revolt. When Titania is herself, Athenian justice is the terrestrial counterpart of a benign personality, and Theseus can put a good face on extenuating the law's sterile force.

This other emphasis, upon justice as the manifestation, in time, of the personality of an often passionate divinity, had my allegiance. For me the parable of the Prodigal Son described a right model: over the world stands a sensitive and loving God, willing and able at critical moments to participate in events; and in the world live men whose duties differ according to their individual conditions. The "modern" concept of what constitutes evidence of an intelligence—deviation from endlessly repeated pattern—had emerged well before 1594. Hooker states it thus: "There is in the will of man naturally that freedom, whereby it is apt to take or refuse any particular object whatsoever being presented unto it."[26] It seemed reasonable that the power to make similar discriminations and the power to exercise similar freedom to decide should belong to the will of God.

Faced with unblinkable evils in London, however, whether our sympathies lay with Calvin, Hooker, or the Pope, we were well acquainted with an age-old difficulty. It was easier to argue a God immense, powerful, just, and rigorous than to argue such a God also benevolent. We came to Oberon's Athens from an often heart-tensing theology, under a God whose magnificent power sometimes appeared menacing.

Like Calvin's picture of God, Oberon is presently active in the world, and as if exemplifying the doctrine of free, unpurchased Grace, he bestows good gifts on human beings to express his own nature, not to requite sacrifice or virtue. At that point the resemblance stops. Oberon is benevolent but no more precise than he is magnificent. More powerful and knowing than any other fairy and much more so than any Athenian, he is far from omniscient or omniscient.

In his Athens questions of justice exhibit a magnitude and complexity corresponding to his tiny stature. When Titania defies him, to be sure, men and the components of nature suffer. They behave inharmoniously with one another and with their own histories. But the pain is milder than in life or tragedy. The machinery of rectification, ponderous as acorn cups and grave as Robin's mischief, is no match for the vision Hal's Lord Chief Justice attempted to inhabit: "The majesty and power of law and justice, / The image of the King" (*Henry IV*, Pt. II, V, ii, 78–79). Given to contrivances rather than great principles, Oberon brings his realm back to order not by force, persuasion, or love, not by directly informing the reason and will, but by a trick—a trick few wise husbands would be tempted to imitate. He is absentminded, whimsical, sometimes mistaken. He demands conscious obedience only from immortal Titania and Robin, not from any man, and moderate are the demands he makes on his queen. While she is defying him the predestinations he rigs are not dependable. When they turn awry he must scheme again. It follows that questions of justice in his world, particularly when inaccurate and mischievous Robin administers his decrees, are bereft of terror.

In God's England in 1595 a man could perform a completely just action when, but only when, his purpose had a spiritual component, when he was consciously obedient to God. Not so in Oberon's Athens. In both realms justice prevails when the right men go to bed with the right women at the right time, when the ruler acts generously toward his subjects and his subjects desire his welfare. But in an Athens where no mortal suspects that Oberon exists there can be no question about obedience to deity. The characters expect just behavior from one another, but we in the audience came to suppose that the men, if not the women, have an extremely limited range in which choice is possible.

A Midsummer Night's Dream did not demand sympathetic terror, the tribute just men command wherever mighty gods endow mortals with capacity for momentous decision and great pain. In England, for example, when Sir Thomas More declined to say his king's words, More's moral stature acquired grandeur appropriate to tragedy. In Shakespeare's own later tragedies we were to see characters confront disasters that have to be endured, fatal problems to which no solution comes. Such characters recall the sustaining strategies of faith: Banquo retreating to the great hand of God; Gertrude offering to a not-yet-ready Hamlet a familiar warm consolation (the burden of the Book of Job and the Ninetieth Psalm) saying, "All that lives must die, / Passing through nature to Eternity" (*Hamlet*, I, ii, 72–73). Sophocles and Homer from their different worlds call upon the heart to cope with shocking events when Antigone defies Creon, when helpless Briseis first receives Agamemnon to her arms. The gods in these stories are mighty, and mortals are vulnerable to spiritual terrors.

A Midsummer Night's Dream invited our minds to vigorous exercise, but did not strain our hearts. It invited us to link a self-including mirth (as wistful handmaiden) to our prevailing tragic sense and contemplate fearsome questions with serenity. Perils to Athenian mortals may be described in dire words, like *death*, but these came through the mind like counters in a game. Playgoers shared with the characters bearable pains, resolvable predicaments, and answerable questions.

In Oberon's world love affords opportunities more complex than an ordinary mind can demand. While Titania is wooing Bottom, her powers are limited to the reach of his imagination with its (for her) despicable though (for us) amusing simplicities. She cannot give what he cannot accept. His desires—for all their bouncing expression—range far down the scale from the aspirations and perceptions that lead to excellent food, a happy bed, and good music. Oberon knows that Titania can make delight flourish in growing things through orderly processes. He expects that she will not long willingly embrace what is conspicuously monstrous and will reject disorder once it has run its course. Welcoming Robin's outrageous prank, he asks mischief itself to help restore Titania. In her right mind she expresses her love for Oberon in the housekeeping of the natural world, in supervising unrigid harmony among the seasons, and in seeing that things go well with flowers, with the begetting and bearing of babies, with song and dance, with rewards for mortal labor, and with heart's good cheer among men and beasts. The self-discipline to which she returns speaks better for her tact in love than Oberon's practical joke speaks for his judgment.

Oberon's is a world which, though its dynamic structures often make asses of men and render human misbehavior more than probable, lends encouragement to a yearning for joy. Some of us in 1595 demanded much from the animist frame of mind. We wanted to know comprehensively, as well as to reduce things and events to essentials. We were laboring toward a moral stance that takes delight in a "sweet disorder," equates virtue with the generation of joy, and presses mankind toward a humane society. Such a moral stance, struggling to be well born and not yet aborted, we felt was congenial with the eye-twinkling vision we saw in Shakespeare's play.

Part Two

The New Learning and Business

VI NATURE AS A NUCLEUS FOR A COMMUNITY OF KNOWLEDGE

Music and poesy use to quicken you.
The mathematics and the metaphysics,
Fall to them as you find your stomach serves you;
No profit grows where is no pleasure ta'en.
In brief, sir, study what you most affect.
                    —*The Taming of the Shrew*, I, i

AS YOU look back at the judicious part of early audiences attending *A Midsummer Night's Dream*, the shape and quality of your own world may prompt you to look with singular respect. Many peoples have desired speed, comforts, and power over nature and society. My contemporaries developed a form of that appalling, fruitful instrument, the human mind operating in a naturalist frame, and they put it to use in industry, trade, and government. You celebrate your debt to us whenever you enjoy your freedom, your laws, your music, your theater, your education, your health, your language, and your sense of humor as well as the interacting structure of your science, technology, and wealth.

We were a part of a great budding European naturalist community whose members were linked by compatible mentalities across space and time, despite differing abilities, dignities, loyalties, economic functions, moral codes, loves, and hates. Although not a formally declared and organized community like the Company of Weavers, English naturalists knew one another's minds through reading and conversation. Those of us who attended Shakespeare's comedy enjoyed the laughter that membership in an audience containing congenial spirits makes possible.

We were far from completely naturalist thinkers. Individual by individual, we exhibited traits of vigorous human beings in a turbulent age. All were ready for Bacon's clean prose, but some of us could endure turgid expositions that will try your stomachs when I offer a small portion. We clung to notions that you dismiss as superstitions and daily endorsed a Christendom whose logic, when it worked, warmed us like sunrise. Had we been pure doctrinaire naturalists we could not have relished so keenly Oberon and Titania's newly created world nor the errors of its unsuperstitious inhabitants.

{85

Yet taking us all together—philosophers, merchants, inventors, manufacturers, physicians, mathematicians, astronomers, lawyers, craftsmen, financiers, musicians, students, sea captains, entrepreneurs—our skills and conquests, our thoughts and actions outside the theater gave England a place to stand and a lever long enough to move the world. We listened, sometimes at first hand if more often at second, to what nature under the rack of experiment had to say. The less famous among us afforded a stimulating audience to the giants on whose shoulders Newton eventually perched. We were not Thomas Huxleys; nor were we Marxists whom no black cat ever startled. But in our rebellious times we functioned as naturalists, no matter what impulses set us to work, no matter how our public words subsequently interpreted our deeds.

In this chapter, as I ask you to review evidence of our community in the new philosophy, I do not want you to know the whole truth about us—just enough to afford adequate contexts so that you may imagine how you might have seen *A Midsummer Night's Dream* had you not only read the books we read but wanted what we wanted and known what we knew about the inhabitants of London and its environs.

II / The Old not Laid Aside, the New Already Tried

If you find it strange that Bacon, Briggs, Dee, Digges, Galileo, Gilbert, Hariot, Harvey, Kepler, Mercator, Napier, and Ralegh felt at home in the circle which their findings were beginning to twist out of round, their stories should at least enable you to credit incongruities in their less-famous brethren. When you remember that brash Sir Walter Ralegh, whose words had earned him accusations of atheism, began his *History of the World* by linking nature with the Bible as a document in theology, saying that God informs men "by his own word and by this visible world," you surely recognize that less daring and perceptive law students, proceeding upon naturalist working assumptions about the nature of things and scheming for wealth with a logic as Euclidean as Niccolo Machiavelli's, could without conscious mendacity publicly endorse the assumptions that led St. Francis to espouse poverty.

Or if we university graduates could without gagging bend our minds and think like Kepler as he constructed orbits to fit hard data but talked as if the orbits were commissioned to proclaim the Holy Trinity,[1] what can you expect of city men who learned to predict events in nature and society at forge and loom, in the Royal Exchange, and through transactions with winds, waves, water rats, and the skills of navigators, but learned their language for nature and passion at church? Donne might get learning and transmute citizens' skills and products into metaphysical conceits, but those without poetic genius were no worse than mortal fools if like Quince and Bottom, they unwittingly constructed a naturalist world and still talked of things other than business in an unreconstructed animist language.

Yet the time was very ripe, and many of my friends were ready to notice disparities between asserted spiritual beliefs and unstated naturalist assumptions that generated daily actions. I will not deny (but we need not dwell on) ugly symptoms of the ripeness—the pre–1595 accusations, persecutions, and riots expressing fear of unfamiliar concepts. Nor shall I dwell on the dark burden in the womb of time—shocking assaults on inquiry such as those that in the seventeenth century cost Giordano Bruno his life and Galileo some of his freedom.[2] In 1595 many men could still greet surprising naturalist words without resentment, and most educated men could still hear discourses on soul without disgust. The time was ripe for Shakespeare's comic mirror, in which we merrily beheld Pyramus and Lysander analytically caricaturing frames of mind we recognized intimately well.

Although nobody took either of the contrasting comic settings in *A Midsummer Night's Dream* for a sober world view, no other accessible model fully satisfied curious men. Historians like E. J. Dijksterhuis who trace the advance of scientific thought treat with special respect epochs that exhibit self-consistent comprehensive paradigms. They admire the great Greeks. Despite Newton's own religious preoccupations, they hail the seventeenth century with its "mechanization of the world picture"[3] and rejoice in its mathematically beautiful model, worth protecting for a while from imprecise, wild, dirty, unique events. They have seen the years of Elizabeth as an untidy approach to the clean, well-lighted age. But if you of the less-confident waning twentieth century can in your imaginations stand inside the sixteenth and see it for itself in its authentic littered condition, rather than see it as a prelude, you may feel at home with its inquiring inhabitants.

If you will attempt to look with eyes like ours at the Athens of *A Midsummer Night's Dream*, laugh with a laughter informed in the perilous ways ours was informed, you will recall traits that distinguish us from the stereotype into which the police would gladly have molded us. You will recall naturalist aspects of our reading, recall our forms of gregariousness, our ways of talking about naturalist problems, our concept of Athens as the fountainhead of natural philosophy, and our grounds for feeling that we bore a resemblance to the ancient Athenians.

In the 1590s more men than ever before knew they wanted that strange, complicating experience of the world which books can bring. The ready presses responded. Although notoriously washed in devotional literature, edified by ethical treatises, titillated by narratives, and deluged with tracts, we devoured works on nature in growing numbers. Latin, German, Dutch, French, and Italian as well as English authors reinforced traditional ideas, but some also reported discoveries, new or revised theories, and the principles on which bold thinkers were operating.[4]

In Volumes V and VI of his *History of Magic and Experimental Science*, Lynn Thorndike displays passages that show promise of the "enlightened" future. W. P. D. Wightman's second volume of *Science and the Renaissance*, "An Annotated Bibliography of the Sixteenth Century Books Relating to the Sciences in the Library of the University of Aberdeen," describes the impressive collection on which rests his "Introduction to the Study of the Emergence of the Sciences in the Sixteenth Century."[5]

The roster of postclassical contributors to the naturalist frame of mind contains names to conjure with: Peter Abelard, Roger

Bacon, Erasmus, Montaigne, Nicholas of Cusa, Paracelsus, Francesco Piccolomini, Pico della Mirandola, Rabelais, Andreas Vesalius, and the avowed inductivist Juan Vives. Instead of reviewing their work I shall in a moment describe some English mathematicians, less famous in later years but familiar to us and influential in 1595. They all still reiterated the name of God, but they cultivated and propagated like a gospel the abstract science that gives language to the naturalist's mind and guides the tools in his hands. Beginning about midcentury and with increasing vehemence they proclaimed its utility. Particularly in the years just before 1595 they were insisting that properties responsive to experimental inquiry can best be phrased in mathematical terms.

Some wrote in Latin, of course, even the astronomer Thomas Digges. Some made foreign works available in English, as when Digges translated Copernicus and Henry Billingsley translated Euclid. But many composed in English accessible to London citizens innocent of classical education. As far back as 1542 Robert Recorde published, as a mildly witty dialogue, his admired and frequently reprinted Arithmetic, *The Ground of Artes*. Recorde's Astronomy, *The Castle of Knowledge*, 1556, follows the pre-Copernican model, and though some applications—to navigation, for example—are practical´ enough, and though there is no ecstatic mysticism, the list of uses for astronomy reveals a bias not wholly materialist: agriculture, law, medicine, divinity—in short, "all the arts."

III / English Mathematicians

In 1585 John Blagrave published *The Mathematical Jewell*, a large book mostly devoted to straightforward mathematical reasoning, notably in geometry. The title page makes a limited appeal to the practical: "compiled and published for the furtherance, as well of Gentlemen and others desirous of speculative knowledge and private practice: as also for the furnishing of such worthy minds, navigators, and travelers, that pretend long voyages, or new discoveries."

Before 1595 Georg Henisch wrote *The Principles of Geometry, Astronomie, and Geographie*, Leonard Digges and Edward

Warsop applied arithmetic and geometry to land measuring, and Thomas Blundeville wrote on arithmetic, trigonometry, astronomy, and navigation. Thomas Hood's *The Use of Both the Globes, Celestiall and Terrestrial*, like Recorde's Arithmetic a dialogue, kept its title-page promise to furnish "most pleasant, and profitable conclusions for the Mariner and generally for those, that are addicted to these kind of mathematical instruments." Valentine Leigh's *The Moste Profitable and Commendable Science of Surveying of Landes, Tenements and Hereditaments* was, as it were, a handbook for landowners. In addition to teaching the surveyor's skill for establishing boundaries and acreage, Leigh expounded laws of property and ways of negotiating with tenants. The only book before 1595 by Dee's best student, Thomas Hariot, whose original accomplishments in algebra, astronomy, and experimentation earned him a high rank in England and among men like Kepler and Galileo, was *A Brief and True Report of the New Found Land of Virginia*, 1588, a lively, mainly statistical summary of resources.[6]

The verbose enthusiasm of some mathematicians, their willingness at times to have their art appear difficult, their emphasis nonetheless upon practical applications, their astonishment that people should be hostile instead of grateful, and their ostentatious religiosity are illustrated in the "Mathematicall Praeface" supplied by Dr. John Dee for Billingsley's translation, 1570.[7] Dee was irritating, fascinating, and for years an influential advocate in fields that developed into true sciences and technologies. However, even on those frequent occasions when he described verifiable phenomena he was recognizably the same man who could be gulled into folly by the alchemist's will-o'-the-wisp. His energies often responded to productive lures, and I want to praise him more than I ridicule him. But if you can be patient for a page or two please listen to his prose. Envisioning a world his mathematics might fit, Dee is not altogether like Pyramus who, caught in such a world, supposes it animist, fit for expression in "poetry." But when we noted that Bottom and his friends have created this Pyramus and this world, we saw Bottom mirroring an incongruity that Dee's preface nakedly illustrates. As Dee extols mathematics, the austere language untouchable by pedantries, posturings, and joyous human desires, he talks as other such people often talked, in a language of religion and passion. As you enrich your ears with a measure or two of Dee's intemperate prose, you may perhaps be able to savor the long familiar, tediously enthusiastic, humorless context of bombast which provoked audiences to laughter when Bottom as Pyramus said, "Approach ye Furies fell, / O fates come, come, cut thread and thrumme, / Quail, crush, conclude, and quell."

After an initial genuflection to Plato and Aristotle, Dee on his second page elevates mathematics to its position in the great scheme of things:

All things which are and have being are found under a triple diversity general. For either they are deemed supernatural, natural, or of a third being. Things supernatural are immaterial, simple, indivisible, incorruptible, and unchangeable. Things natural are material, compounded, divisible, corruptible, and changeable. Things supernatural are of the mind only comprehended; things natural of the sense exterior are able to be perceived. In things natural probability and conjecture hath place; but in things supernatural chief demonstration and most sure science is to be had. By which properties and comparisons of these two, more easily may be described the state, condition, nature, and property of those things which we before termed of a third being: which, by a peculiar name also, are called *Things Mathematical*. For these, being in a manner middle between things supernatural and natural, are not so absolute and excellent as things supernatural, nor yet so base and gross as things natural: but are things immaterial, and nevertheless by material things able somewhat to be signified. And though their particular images by art are aggregable and divisible, yet the Forms notwithstanding are constant, unchangeable, untransformable, and incorruptible. Neither of the sense can they at any time be perceived or judged, nor yet, for all that, in the royal mind of man first conceived. But, surmounting the imperfection of conjecture, weening, and opinion and coming short of high intellectual conception, are the Mercurial fruit of Dianoetical discourse, in perfect imagination subsisting.

Quaint shades of Plato!

In praise of quantification Dee chants that number exists first in the mind of the Creator. Calling on Plato to witness the close alliance between wisdom and skill in numbers, he announces that of all sciences, next to theology, arithmetic (in which he includes algebra) "is the most divine, most pure, most ample and general, most profound, most subtle, most commodious, and most necessary." (A iv) He sees in the science of magnitude (his word for geometry and trigonometry) a glory only slightly less stunning.

Having discharged his duty to talk passionately about mathematics in a God-ordained world, Dee turns to practical problem solving. He thus joins other English mathematicians in lengthening—and distorting—the shadow of Archimedes rather than Plato. By the arts of number and magnitude, he says, men carry on effective warfare and accurate navigation. Arithmetic guides merchant, goldsmith, physician, and lawyer. With geometry one may measure things (kegs of beer, cities, the heavens) and make plane, spherical, and topographical maps. Despite an outlandish terminology, Dee's list of mathematical arts is as naturalist as you please: gunnery, transport, irrigation, mining, the lifting of heavy weights, physiology, anatomy, time telling, and architecture, and music.

He sometimes goes beyond practical problems and sounds as interested as a physicist in what experiment may disclose:

Pneumatithmie demonstrateth by close hollow geometrical figures (regular and irregular) the strange properties (in motion or stay) of the water, air, smoke, and fire, in their continuity and as they are joined to the elements next them. This art, to the natural philosopher, is very profitable: to prove that vacuum or emptiness is not in the world; and that all nature abhorreth it so much that, contrary to law, the elements will move or stand. As, water to ascend rather than, between him and air, space or place should be left more than (naturally) that quantity of air requireth or can fill. Again, water to hang and not descend rather than by descending to leave emptiness at his back. The like is of fire and air: they will descend when either their continuity should be dissolved or their next element forced from them. And as they will not be extended to discontinuity, so they will not, nor yet of man's force can be, pressed or pent in space not sufficient and answerable to their bodily substance. Great force and violence will they use, to enjoy their natural right and liberty. Hereupon, two or three men together, by keeping air under a great cauldron and forcing the same down, orderly, may without harm descend to the sea bottom and continue there a time, etc. Where, note how the thicker element (as the water) giveth place to the thinner, in manner, etc. Pumps and all manner of bellows have their ground of this art, and many other strange devices, as Hydraulics, organs going by water, etc. Of this feat (called commonly pneumatica) goodly works are extant, both in Greek and Latin. With old and learned school men it is called *Scientia de Plano and vacuo*. (C iiii v—D i r)

In his writing and in all the other aspects of the social dimension of his naturalist activity, Dee indefatigably promoted his three mathematical passions: pure mathematics, mathematics as the key to wonderful secrets of nature, and above all, mathematics as a tool for men at work. And so he contributed to making this *triune* interest (if I may perpetrate a Dee-ism) a commonplace among English pursuers of natural knowledge, especially among those London citizen prototypes of Bottom who were about to establish Gresham College.

Nearly all the people with whom I could converse about naturalist matters were vivid individuals, many of them pugnaciously self-assertive. But probably the most important fact about us was that we could communicate with one another and did so hungrily, compulsively, diligently. We had a sense of identity as a community solely because we understood one another. It is for my present purposes a subsidiary point that this community was a necessary condition for the emergence of the modern world. The understanding of *A Midsummer Night's Dream* that I am offering you could not have possessed me had I not known that the play was speaking similarly to a host of people only a small fraction of whom I had ever laid eyes on. Their questions about the world and their ways of worrying made them friends of mine for whom I can speak. The devices of communication that sustained our identity almost define our identity. They were the same devices by which the ancient Athenian naturalist community came into being, nourished itself, and extended itself through time and space.

IV / The Social Dimension of Naturalist Activity

We wrote letters to one another. Although some letters deserved to be called epistles, imitating speculative, propositional epistles of men like Plato, Aristotle, and Epicurus, the letters that promoted our more practical naturalism usually described phenomena we had observed and things we had done to manipulate nature. Had the ballad entitled "Bottom's Dream" actually been written it would have illustrated the motives if not the occasions that characterized our correspondence. John Dee was not the only man who wrote hundreds of letters. Investigators in particular busily wrote them, as your scientists still do even while they fill journals and disseminate offprints. Through letters the best of us discussed world-shaking developments with one another and with opposite numbers on the Continent, as when in 1572 the new star in Cassiopeia exhibited its shocking remoteness. A host of us, more modest letter writers, recorded and circulated our observations of uncommon events at sea, in the air, and in the fields.[8]

V /
Conversation

Like the ancient Athenians we cultivated our sense of community with face-to-face talk. "Conversation," greatly praised, was not strictly limited to spoken words, nor its practice to dabblers in natural philosophy. Robert Parsons, for example, echoed a conventional imperative: "Wittily said Aristotle in the second chapter of his first book of politics, that he which flieth to live in society is either Deus aut Bellua, a god or a beast; for that either he doth it because he hath no need of any, which is proper to God, or else for that he will do good to none, and feeleth not that natural instinct, which man hath to live in conversation, which is a sign rather of a beast than of a man."[9] But when moralists called life in society the nurse of virtues they were urging us to talk.

In the first Book of *The Civile Conversation of M. Steeven Guazzo*, which George Pettie translated and published in 1581, Annibal says, "If the learned and students love solitariness for lack of their like, yet they naturally love the company of those which are their like: in so much that many of them have travelled far with great labour to speak with other learned men, whose books they had at home in their houses." [10] In claiming triumphs for discourse Annibal is not more modest than mathematicians: "Neither can a learned man assure himself of his learning, until he meet with other learned men, and by discoursing and reasoning with them, be ascertained of his sufficiency. Whereby it seemeth to me very clear, that conversation is the beginning and end of knowledge." [11]

Annibal thus flouts the great Hebrew pronouncement that "the fear of the Lord is the beginning of wisdom." He justifies Bacon's jest: "Atheists will ever be talking of . . . their opinion." [12] He continues: "But above all other things the commendable controversies which arise amongst learned men have most force to quicken the spirits. For by disputing they learn, and that which they learn in that manner, they understand best, they expound best, and remember best. And while they dispute by lively reasons, endeavoring to get the upper hand each of other, the perfect knowledge of things is come by, and thereupon it is commonly said that disputation is the sifter out of the truth. And for so much as the truth is taken from the common consent and opinions of men, those opinions cannot be known but by conversation and company." [13]

I remember when I read these words in Guazzo I underlined them and jotted approving comments in the margin. My memory of Guazzo and my appetite for conversation imparted a wry quality to my laughter when I heard two classic models of conversation in *A Midsummer Night's Dream*. I was somewhat prepared for the disputation between Theseus and Hippolyta near the end of the play when Hippolyta advances the notion that the stories of the lovers might be evidence for something authentic and is promptly squelched by Theseus' magnificent *argumentum ad personam* about lunatics and lovers. The conversation could hardly be called a "sifter out of truth." Nor could the conversation between Hermia and Lysander early in the play. Lysander completely persuades himself and Hermia that since the course of true love never did run smooth it cannot. Hermia draws the impregnable inference that lovers must practice patience. Lysander agrees and with an incredible *therefore* proposes an elopement. So much for the proposition that "conversation is the beginning and the end of knowledge." Of course *A Midsummer Night's Dream* did not put an end to conversation, certainly not mine.

A twentieth-century scientist still cultivates identity with other scientists through conversation. He might select more temperate phrases than "perfect knowledge of things" and "the truth." He finds joy in discovering fresh data and devising models to bring them under discipline. Nevertheless he participates in "the common consent and opinions" of his own kind of men. The English physicist John Ziman, amplifying his title *Public Knowledge*, says that "the objective of Science is a consensus of rational opinion." He goes on:

The scientific enterprise is corporate. It is not merely, in Newton's incomparable phrase, that one stands on the shoulders of giants, and hence can see a little farther. Every scientist sees through his own eyes—and also through the eyes of his predecessors and colleagues. It is never one individual that goes through all the steps of the logico-inductive chain; it is a group of individuals, dividing their labour but continuously and jealously checking each other's contributions. The cliché of scientific prose betrays itself: "Hence *we* arrive at the conclusion that . . ." The audience to which scientific publications are addressed is not passive; by its cheering or booing, its bouquets or brickbats, it actively controls the substance of the communications that it receives.[14]

In and near London, centers of germinal conversation thrived on achieved consensus and promoted our sense of community. One was Dr. John Dee's home at Mortlake. Long before 1595 Dee had gambled away dignity and prestige on a disastrous mission to Bohemia, hoping to make England rich by importing the secret of making gold, and a mob had plundered his library and array of instruments. But many of us still remembered the great years when influential people, including the queen, had visited there, and brilliant young men like Thomas Digges and Thomas Hariot had made themselves his disciples.[15] Dee's "poor house" as he called it, was not just like the ancients' Academy, the Lyceum, and Epicurus' garden, but we thought of those places when we went out to Mortlake. And I thought of Mortlake when I heard the conversation-filled minutes before and during "Pyramus and Thisby" in Theseus' palace.

Sir Walter Ralegh, one of the old Mortlake group, had by 1592 assembled his own "schoole of Atheisme." There I met Chapman and Marlowe, a ship's captain named Lawrence Keymes, who was also an amateur in geography and mathematics, and the Earls of Northumberland and Derby, still interested in alchemy. The notoriety of this group derived not from writings but from the way some of us talked rashly outside the circle.[16]

At the Inns of Court, each inn housing its own lively community, conversation flowed over a multitude of topics in addition to litigation, power, and precedents. During Christmas revels at Gray's Inn, 1594–95, a speech composed for "The Second Councillor, advising the Study of Philosophy" urged not metaphysics or ethics but natural philosophy.[17] Francis Bacon was in residence at the time, and the speech can show you the kind of naturalist speculation that interested us. Bacon composed *The Advancement of Learning* some ten years later, but already he was urging that new findings, or at any rate "such of them as conduce to the capturing of the correspondence of men of wit and the cleansing of the threshing-floor of minds be popularized and spread abroad by word of mouth."[18]

The Double Helix describes a twentieth-century variant on the kind of intellectual profit we in 1595 sought from community in operation. To win his Nobel Prize James Watson ransacked the minds of men and women better informed than he.[19] Formulations worked with and against one another in his and their busy heads, accumulating congenial and eliminating uncongenial elements until—how should I put it? until he and his closest colleague achieved? until their scientific community achieved? until conversation achieved? until nature achieved? until God revealed? a usable model of the DNA molecule.

In 1595 students of natural philosophy had not achieved the detached purity of aim that marks twentieth-century science. We expected philosophical conversation, like experiment, to have results theoretical, practical, and moral—results that could engage the total allegiance of "men of wit." It was to achieve a comprehensively powerful instrument that Bacon was working out his model for inquiry into Nature. His dream of a method by which people might hear Nature tell her secrets persisted almost to the time of Watson. Maybe some are still trying for it. Nobody wrote a ballad about it but philosophers paid appropriate homage to Bacon's dream when they organized the Royal Society. A socially structured and manageable if far-from-precise method operates in laboratories and conferences around your world.

VI /
Institutions

In the twentieth century the institution where scientists most readily find working community is the established university. Naturalist rebels accused sixteenth-century Oxford and Cambridge of a mind-shackling conservatism, and some historians of science have concurred. Aside from remembering that the authentic reactionaries damned any university as an Athens, meaning a hotbed of atheism, and noticing that many distinguished naturalist thinkers attended Cambridge, let me shrug off the job of vindication and look at group efforts in London.

Obviously I find Thorndike right when he suggests that persistent correspondence among observers of nature prepared the way for scientific societies and their formally cooperative investigations,[20] but already during the latter half of the sixteenth century men in and about London were busy attempting to institutionalize the new learning and propagate it in an acceptable context. They organized lecture courses. Marie Boas mentions the series by Robert Recorde about midcentury and refers to numerous subsequent series extending into the seventeenth century. Early instances were public lectures on anatomy sponsored by the Company of Barbers and Surgeons and lectures on surgery at the Royal College of Physicians.[21]

Two enterprises marked 1572, the same year when, as my parents told me, I saw the astonishing nova. Archbishop Matthew Parker founded a Society of Antiquaries, a far cry, indeed, from the Royal Society.[22] The other enterprise produced no institution, but it did leave a document that illustrates our naturalist thinking. Sir Humphrey Gilbert, Ralegh's great half brother, petitioned Queen Elizabeth for "the erection of an Academy in London for education of her Majesty's wards and others the youth of nobility and gentlemen." Instruction proposed by Sir Humphrey included arithmetic, geometry, fortification, cosmography, astronomy, navigation, ship handling, shipbuilding, natural philosophy, medicine, and surgery. The faculty would employ scale models for instruction, engage in experimentation, and (nearly a century before the Royal Society initiated the practice) prepare research reports. The following passage is typical:

This physician shall continually practice together with the natural philosopher, by the fire and otherwise, to search and try out the secrets of nature, as many ways as they possibly may. And shall be sworn once every year to deliver into the treasurer's office, fair and plain written on parchment, without equivocations or enigmatical phrases, under their hands, all those their proofs and trials made within the forepassed year, together with the true event of things, and all other necessary accidents growing thereby, to the end that their successors may know both the way of their working, and the event thereof, the better to follow the good, and avoid the evil, which in time must of force bring great things to light, if in chemistry there be any such things hidden.[23]

Hostile Spanish gestures in 1588 produced a situation illustrating scientists' propensity for converting military need into academic opportunity. To lay a foundation for training in artillery and navigation, needed by captains of a hastily raised militia, aldermen and the lord mayor appointed Thomas Hood to a lectureship in mathematics and astronomy. They opened the doors to all applicants. It was my good fortune that the emergency, for educational purposes, lasted three or four years after the Armada had become a theme of glory in our memories.[24]

In 1595 naturalist thought was even less precise than today. The most advanced theorists expected that mere accumulated instances of nature's behavior, seen together, would reveal new

VII / Problem Solving

and interesting general propositions. Their notion of postulates
and controls was primitive compared with yours. But happily
their intuitions were sometimes powerful, especially when a
practical need, as in navigation, limited the data and brought a
problem into focus.

With all our shortcomings the best of us had a growing skill in
naturalist problem solving, as witness our mathematicians and
especially Dee's preface. In *A Midsummer Night's Dream* the
aristocratic Athenians approached no problem in the distinctive
naturalist way, so far as I noticed, but the artisans outrageously
did when they had to set their stage. A case can be made that
actors representing things other than people in Babylon do no
more violence to propriety than actors representing forces of
nature by calling themselves Oberon, Titania, and Robin. But
the sense of mutilated decorum was vivid when actors played
the parts of conspicuously soulless Wall, Moonshine, and Lion.
The device commented upon the degree to which we naturalists, whether we were philosophers or inventive craftsmen,
really offended classical and traditional canons of intellectual
decency whenever we attacked a problem in our new fashion.

VIII / Athens   In the substance of their thought as well as in devices of com-
Imitated   munication, the ancient Greeks supplied the clearest precedent
for a naturalist community fit to relish a comedy in which the
wisdom of the gods themselves is questionable. Disseminated
by hearsay, central in the curriculum of universities, and
cherished in libraries, the ideas originally embalmed in Greek
books were the naturalist statements known to us in 1595. Pre-
Socratic logic and models of matter, motion, and the structure of
worlds were accessible not only in Latin versions of Aristotle's
Physics and in Plato but in commentaries only some of which
had been badly distorted by Arabian and Western minds. Accessible were Latin and Greek texts of Diogenes Laertius' gossipy
Lives of Eminent Philosophers and the discussion of Epicurus in
Lucretius' *On the Nature of Things*. Even in St. Augustine of
Hippo, who sought to confute non-Christian models, we found
accounts always provocative and not always inaccurate.

We knew that before Aquinas made the complete world model Aristotle spoke about a Prime Mover. We remembered that in Aristotle's Athens mortals might take an interest in the Prime Mover if they pleased, but the regard was not even acknowledged. In Shakespeare's Athens we observed Oberon taking an interest in mortals who do not acknowledge his existence.

We knew that Anaximander used the word *god* but that his gods are systems of matter and force, not personalities such as Pyramus thinks he talks to. We thought of Anaximander when rambunctious Titania and self-confident Oberon quarrel but not remorselessly. In Anaximander's model the only action describable in moral terms is the behavior of systems which have separated themselves from a primordial undifferentiated something. These, conceived as having done injustice by acquiring distinct existence, conflict with and eventually destroy one another and so subside into their amorphous condition.[25]

Democritus' somewhat sophisticated and notorious model sat ready in our consciousness as we watched the "rude mechanicals" display an absurd Babylon for Pyramus and Thisby to die in. The atomist, we knew, reasons that worlds (and all things and events in any world) come about from fortuitous concatenations of forces, objects, and time: each segment of a world obeys natural laws, but the laws, like those in Pyramus' Babylon, are never coordinated by any intelligence.

Epicurus follows Democritus in asserting that all information comes through the senses (vision, hearing, touch, and so on) but adds that knowledge is intelligible only to those who have been prepared by prior experience. One way to translate his word for this preparation is "preconception."[26] We recognized that Epicurus lurked behind Helena's comment that "Love lookes not with the eyes, but with the minde"; behind Hermia's wish that Egeus might look with her eyes; behind Theseus' speech on tricks of the imagination that can convert a bush into a bear; and indeed behind the whole pattern that shows Athenians and Babylonians, each group in its peculiar fashion, seeing the world only as they are prepared to see it—and seeing it wrong.

Acknowledged living enemies of God, gods, and spirits were even scarcer in England in 1595 than those other dreadful people, Jews and Catholics. Only atheist Greeks—and that from the pages of old books—were still openly ridiculing stories of gods, still proclaiming a naturalist world that would eventually breed Thomas A. Edison. The ancients stood in stark contrast with more recent writers like Guillaume du Bartas, who proclaimed a world redeemed by Christ and who, condemning Democritus, preferred to remember God saying, "Let there be light."[27]

IX / A New Athenian Community   We felt that our London resembled Athens in the development of an intellectual mood more important than either devices or specific doctrines. The resemblance bred an allegiance that continues in your own universities. Alfred North Whitehead and Thomas Henry Huxley, among others, have tried to name the forerunners of scientific thought. Huxley said, "In truth, it is in the Greek world that we must seek, not only the predecessors but the spiritual progenitors, of modern men of science."[28] Huxley was talking about Euclid, Hipparchus, Archimedes, and especially Galen. Whitehead talks about other Greeks:

> The pilgrim fathers of the scientific imagination as it exists today are the great tragedians of ancient Athens, Aeschylus, Sophocles, Euripides. Their vision of fate, remorseless and indifferent, urging a tragic incident to its inevitable issue, is the vision possessed by science. Fate in Greek tragedy becomes the order of nature in modern thought. . . . The essence of dramatic tragedy is not unhappiness. It resides in the solemnity of the remorseless working of things. This inevitableness of destiny can only be illustrated by incidents which in fact involve unhappiness. For it is only by them that the futility of escape can be made evident in the drama. This remorseless inevitableness is what pervades scientific thought. The laws of physics are the decrees of fate.[29]

Whether we Elizabethans studied our Greek lessons while seeking models for the natural world or while responding to Homer, parsing the propositions of mathematics or the pulses of poetry, we looked with a sense of community back to the city we deemed the center of Greek civilization. We saw the ancient

Athenians speaking with one another in common modes of curiosity as well as in a common language across an impressive span of years. Aeschylus, Euripides, and Sophocles were the products of a community theater. They looked at the consequences of arrogance, and when they launched an action with a persuasively predictable end they exhibited a mentality disciplined to the same model of nature that belonged to Archimedes, years later, when he contemplated the behavior of his body and its bath water just before he scurried out declaiming the naked predictive truth.

Besides the great tragedians there were Leucippus, Democritus, Socrates, and Plato. The natural philosophers taught the tragedians, the tragedians taught the philosophers. Both groups taught those sons of Hephaistos who devised mechanisms,[30] and learned from them, though not so much as we learned from our craftsmen. Through such interaction of minds the great Greek community came into existence and persisted.[31] The story of Archimedes' "Eureka" is most credible if we suppose that he bathed in company and that in the bath he customarily conversed with other bathing Syracusans and profited by social pressure to make sense in the Athenian mode. The great old Athenian community thrived on the disparity between its members, some as unaware of gods as Lysander, others as confident of conscious gods as Pyramus. But most of them, like most of us, sometimes followed remorseless naturalist necessities and sometimes remembered Asklepios.

Of course Englishmen in 1595, though we imitated the ancients, were in significant ways different. I shan't quarrel with Whitehead's moving suggestion that the laws of physics are in the Greek sense eternal, universal, and analogous to the terrors of the human heart. However, we were learning to think of the laws in contexts less Aeschylean. We were training ourselves for the limited statement, fit for the ritual of experiment, in the tradition of Archimedes. Archimedes' solution to Hero's question about whether his crown was pure gold or an alloy was a statement not limited in time or space—but limited in that it addressed a single practical question about an insoluble solid,

and limited in that it fully phrased all the observable components and relationships of the question and nothing else: mass,
displaced water, and volume.

Galileo's thinking about "impetus" illustrates the tendency of
our time to come closer and closer to Archimedes' kind of question. In 1592 Galileo was, like the rest of us, still Aristotelian
enough to regard impetus as something existing in a body as a
cause of its motion—a sort of extension of the First Cause. By
1604 he preferred to limit his thoughts about motion to measur-
able properties of the body itself and the forces applied to it.[32] In
1595 English philosophical thinkers who with the help of
craftsmen were learning to ask what happens to a specific thing
under a specific set of circumstances and what use can be made
of the answer were making our whole community ready to respond to the later Galileo and, before that, ready to respond to
naturalist Lysander.

We who frequented plays in 1595 felt a link with ancient
Athenians who attended first performances of Aeschylus and
Aristophanes and with Syracusans who bathed near Archimedes. To scratch the itch for imperial dominion we spoke of
New Troy and Rome. When we speculated about ways to understand and control nature, we invoked the home city of philosophical Greece, which we felt was not Syracuse, not Alexandria, but Athens. To our ears "Athens" sounded an overtone
of just enough peril to sharpen its note of delight.

People little acquainted with research scientists sometimes
think of them only as grave faces. But consult your Michael
Polanyi,[33] who speaks of the twentieth-century investigator's
"elation" over a scientific "discovery." The climactic research
event, to the investigator and to colleagues who can use it, apparently feels like opening Chapman's Homer, even when they
dryly call it not a discovery but a construct. If naturalist inquiry
was joyous when Archimedes uttered his shout and is joyous in
the twentieth century, in the dawn that was 1595 it was bliss to
be a live naturalist. Every glimpse provided by exercise of intellectual powers freshly rediscovered from ancient Greece, and

freshly applied, was exciting. We saw in Shakespeare's Athens a comic city that commented on our natural, not to say our spiritual, home.

The ancient Athenian audience that first witnessed events in *Prometheus Bound* felt invited to understand decrees of the very fate they must contend with in their actual lives. That is not far from the way Englishmen understood events in the Book of Job—as revealing a God we must endure. At *A Midsummer Night's Dream* we felt a different invitation. Though we learned how it was to live under Oberon, we did not deem ourselves called upon except jestingly to consider whether any event outside the play was subject to the laws of Oberon's world. As a new breed of naturalists we knew how to put a finite limit on the reach of our thoughts. Fortunately for comedy, we had not fully learned the lesson.

Matthew Arnold, giving his inaugural lecture in the Poetry Chair at Oxford, "On the Modern Element in Literature," contrasts the Age of Pericles, exemplified by a passage from Thucidides' *History of the Peloponnesian War*, with the Elizabethan Age, exemplified by a piece of legendary animism in Ralegh's *History of the World*. He judges the two ages by "the critical power . . . possessed by the majority of intelligent men," and finds the Age of Pericles superior. Many of us would ruefully have agreed. Arnold complains about our credulity as if the Pericleans were as judiciously skeptical as Thucidides claims to be, though he quotes Thucidides' complaint about his fellow Pericleans' "habit of *uncritical* reception of current ['half-fabulous'] stories." I know I flout Arnold's judgment when I claim that many Elizabethans were gifted with keen enough powers of "rational appreciation" to find in *A Midsummer Night's Dream* a comment on human credulity as discerning as Thucidides' and incomparably more sweet tempered. When I read Thucidides I resolved to take a sturdy position on the side of disinterested assessment of the evidence. I came away from Shakespeare's comedy quoting in laughter, "Lord, what fooles these mortals bee!" I felt more than usual kindness towards mortal fools. And during those moments I meant to include among the objects of my kind thoughts my unreflective acquaintances, my philosophical friends, and myself.[34]

Urgencies felt by people like Thucidides in the ancient Athenian community forged intellectual bonds. Their thoughts occurred partly because they knew their words were understood by Greek minds in a Greek way. In 1595 Shakespeare's play came to an English community of minds, shaped on a similar anvil but to a different and fearfully potent design that was part Greek, part Hebrew, and part sheer British. We in that community, predestinating the era of technology and science but not yet dominated by a Greek mathematical logic which would find probability a concept hard to tolerate, were ready for *A Midsummer Night's Dream*—ready to understand it in our English way.

VII PERCEPTIONS OF COMIC WORLD MODELS

There's not the smallest orb which thou behold'st
But in his motion like an angel sings,
Still quiring to the young-ey'd cherubins.
                    —*The Merchant of Venice*, V, i

This is the excellent foppery of the world, that, when we
are sick in fortune,—often the surfeits of our own
behaviour,—we make guilty of our disasters the sun,
the moon, and stars.
                    —*King Lear*, I, ii

IN THE London of 1595 great questions were stirring— inquiries into nature and into new and dangerous ways of knowing nature—and our minds reflected all the diversities they were encountering. We had a taste for paradoxes and antitheses, though we knew that such phrasings were often oversimplifications. We liked the pair on which Francis Bacon played a series of variations. One version of his essay "Of Atheism" begins, "I had rather believe all the fables of the Legend, and the Talmud, and the Alcoran, than that this universal frame is without a mind." His "Of Superstition" begins, "It were better to have no opinion of God at all, than such an opinion as is unworthy of him."

If naturalist Lysander and animist Pyramus mirrored us analytically, Hamlet would later mirror part of our complexity. When we heard that troubled prince put naturalist thought in its less-than-royal place, "There are more things in heaven and earth, Horatio, / Than are dreamt of in our philosophy," (I,v, 166–67) we were not astonished at his insistence upon spiritual forces, since he is at that moment heeding his father's ghost. When we saw him devise "The Mousetrap" to pluck the heart out of Claudius' mystery, we saw him conducting an experiment recognizably naturalist, though without adequate controls.

We delighted in *A Midsummer Night's Dream* for presenting not a single but a double antithesis: four world models, each commenting on all the others. We saw at once the two contrasted worlds through which the Athenians and the Babylonians move and the false models they implicitly believe in. Initially we recognized these worlds only as comic reflections of what passed for cosmologies in the minds of four sets of living people: untroubled optimistic Christians, superstitious simpletons, philosophers we admired, and the makers of bugaboos to scare folk into religion. It was our triumph and our woe that the four world

{109

models and the corresponding four ways of thinking, mutually incompatible as they looked, really reflected ourselves—reflected both the happy moments when we thought in only one way and the less happy moments when diverse ways of thinking and diverse models inharmoniously occupied our minds. More easily than Wordsworth we could at times hear old Triton blow his wreathed horn, though we had resolutely decided to banish superstition from our minds. We remembered a childhood practice of conversing (as if with playmates) with things just as far down the chain of being as cobwebs and walls. After we grew up we sometimes believed, as Lysander does, that the maturing of people follows childhood as naturally as the fall of rain. We remembered the moment when our minds had been first excited by Democritus' laughter at superstitions. It left us feeling alien and chilly in a simplified world.

A world earless as a wall, mindless as moonshine, and subject to accelerating accident may appear intrinsically no more horrendous than your second law of thermodynamics and the intriguing proposition that the starry night, the suffering of your hearts, and your beautiful children are essentially bundles of jiggling inanimate particles, or maybe just jiggles. Morticians of four centuries have so well insulated your hearts from your minds that perhaps you now require an act of imagination to respond with the full comic shock, linked so firmly and distantly with prime terror, that Pyramus' dead world delivered to us. A second-rate horror is machinelike man in a machinelike world or even rebellious man in a satanic world. The first-rate horror is a world whose purposeless driving forces afford accidental coincidences that trick imaginative man into interpreting them as parts of a plan wrought and sustained by a cosmic intelligence.

The comical tragedy mirroring this horror was the ultimate testing ground of our sense of community, for no one laughed a lonely laughter. We knew well why Athens was the right city for the comedy. It was right because of its unworshiping inhabitants and its unworshiped diminutive neo-Olympians—despite the superficially contrary evidence of St. Paul on Mars Hill. Our laughter at the unexamined assumptions of the comic Athenians and Babylonians ironically expressed the discernment we had learned from the real Athenian atheists. We took wry pride that we could recall with detachment our own headstrong moments. We began to feel that men sharing naturalist thought make up a stubborn instance of order in a questionable world. We reflected that this order was not enforced by any power other than mind meeting mind. In the face of the picture of chaos, it was comforting to be laughing in concert with like-minded men dispersed here and there through the audience.

When we saw Bottom playing the role of Pyramus, who like Lysander leaves his city for love, we began to think of correspondences between Bottom and Lysander. Bottom's successes are set over against his metaphysical ignorance in every role. In his own person as Bottom the Weaver, citizen, he achieves success as a tragic actor without knowing what his play means. I want to talk later about our perception of Bottom as exhibiting an unphilosophical citizen's spectacular capability to achieve technical successes without knowing or really caring how his activity fits his world. But now I am remembering Bottom as a lover, loved by Thisby and unaware that Babylon is a soulless world. I am remembering him in his translated form, loved by Titania though he remains unaware that spirits rule Athens. His lover's role in both cities reinforced our understanding that the particular texture of love's rough course is a function of the world the lover inhabits.

II / Bottom and Lysander

Lysander too is a successful lover, and he too is ignorant of his world. In both respects he is like the other two Athenian loving men. We laughed at the Athenians' ignorance quite differently from the way we laughed at the Babylonians'. Pyramus and Thisby so crassly ignore actualities that they looked not at all like real people. Thisby was gone before we could love and pity her. Our laughter at Lysander and his friends was a laughter of happier identification. Their fate lies near heart's desire. We felt a special kindness for the Athenian women, who lay plans as if they have world enough and time. Hermia plans marriage. She keeps Lysander at arm's length until lovemaking has what she regards as its proper context, and the outcome justifies her. She does not know about Oberon, but the law of her heart, which she obeys, is right for the world he rules.

When we were reminded by event after event that male Athenians not only mistake the quality and structure of their world but also mistake the individual people they should know best, we were touched in a tender place. They exemplify the danger most dreaded by naturalist thinkers. When we beheld Egeus and with him Theseus irrationally tyrannizing over Hermia, we of course saw a reflection of ancient Athenians and our own Londoners in self-willed family and civil authority. Egeus, trusting his eyes when he sees Demetrius preferable, by the margin of Hermia's life, to a Lysander who obviously tots up to the same value, might be dismissed as a Plautine old man who sets the play in motion. But Lysander's eyes when he prefers now Hermia, now Helena, and now again Hermia, are no better than old eyes. He sees only what he is, for whatever reason, predisposed to see and cannot be counted on to see the actuality before his eyes.

Your experimental scientists, realizing that their data is acquired through the senses, interpose machines whenever they can and profess an ever vigilant laboratory discipline. But in 1595 fallibility of the senses made us question the whole naturalist approach to truth, and I am not sure we were altogether foolish. We observed that when Lysander justifies his infatuation for Helena with talk about man's growth to reason, he proceeds on the naturalist assumption that human conduct is "determined entirely by the organic structure and needs characteristic of the human species."[1] At a time when he is compelled by Oberon's eyedrops he says to Helena, comparing her with Hermia,

> The will of man is by his reason swai'd:
> And reason saies you are the worthier maide.
> Things growing are not ripe, untill their season:

So I, being young, till now ripe not to reason.
And touching now, the point of humane skill,
Reason becomes the Marshall to my will.

These lovely words that juice of the little western flower renders nonsensical accurately phrase doctrines long known and respected by naturalists. Somewhere near the time *A Midsummer Night's Dream* went on the boards Richard Hooker published the first volume of *The Laws of Ecclesiastical Polity*. In the seventh section of the first book he says, "Reason is the director of man's Will by discovering in action what is good," and then in a sequence that Lysander follows he immediately thinks of immature people "which are not as yet come unto those years whereat they may have right Reason." Hooker, who did not trust reason alone, knew that the doctrines of growth and readiness come from the Greeks, and if he kept his sense of humor when he attended Shakespeare's play he too laughed merrily at the great Athenian pronouncement coming, without the theological modification he gave it, from the lips of enchanted naturalist Lysander.[2]

Lysander's words have a philosophical ring. Here and when earlier he has talked about frustrations that beset true love, his position is recognizable: natural laws are not edicts of gods or fairies but inferences from recurring and therefore predictable events. Though he and Demetrius eventually love happily because Oberon wants their mistresses happy, he reasons as if the Athenian heaven were as deserted as the night over doomed Pyramus and Thisby. Utterly unaware as he is of alternatives, we could not say that he *rejects* the gods of his world. No sane Englishman in the sixteenth century was as ignorant of the Christian God as Lysander was ignorant of Oberon, so that Lysander mirrored no live people. We saw him representing a frame of mind, a pure version of the stereotype which hostile citizens saw when they looked at university students and law students.

We laughed at Lysander sympathetically when he mistakenly assumes that he knows the springs of his own conduct. Yet the sympathy comically imperiled us. "It is Margaret you mourn for," says Gerard Manley Hopkins to the child Margaret, who grieves without knowing quite why. "It is Margaret I laugh at," said—or ought to have said—my earlier, advanced-thinking Margaret under her breath as she sat beside me.

III / Playgoers of London and Athens and the Closed Book of Nature

The invitation to see our critical opinions mirrored in aristocratic Athenians watching "Pyramus and Thisby" differed from invitations offered by means of stage audiences at *Love's Labour's Lost* and *Hamlet*. At *Love's Labour's Lost*, like every playgoer who had been bored by classroom pedantry, I accepted Holofernes' clumsy syntax and pretentious diction as an excuse to join the King of Navarre and his friends in ridiculing a character who to my eye caricatures the pedantry of a bookworm king. In a later audience watching Hamlet watching the king watching a stylized "Murder of Gonzago" I was impelled to join with the furious prince and accept as proof of Claudius' guilt a piece of evidence nobody would be justly hanged for. The invitation at *A Midsummer Night's Dream* felt neither so bald as Holofernes' nor so bold as Hamlet's. Many faceted and elaborate, it flattered us even as it poked its fun. Laughter at Lysander and Demetrius as they laugh at Pyramus and Thisby was the momentous laughter provoked by *A Midsummer Night's Dream*. As we joined the Athenians in laughing at the animist lovers in a soulless world, we remembered incident after incident when these same sophisticates have displayed their own mistaken view of their own world.

We recognized numerous small correspondences between Pyramus' story and Lysander's, each recalling to us—but not to the Athenians—the spirit-dominated Athenian world. Moonshine, walking about in Babylon, recalled the ubiquitous Athenian moon: Theseus and Hippolyta's references to the moon as a timekeeper, Theseus invoking the moon to threaten Hermia with sterility, and the whole moonlit night in the Athenian wood. Snug, playing the lion who frightens Thisby but does not frighten the Athenian ladies, recalled Athenian Bottom, fitted with the head of another beast, frightening his companions but not Titania. Theseus' remark when Bottom in the role of Pyramus keels over dead reminded us of the ass's head Bottom lays in Titania's lap: "With the helpe of a Surgeon," says Theseus, "he might yet recover, and yet proove an Asse."

We remembered the substance of Hermia's naturalist disquisition on ears and eyes as she hails straying Lysander:

> Darke night, that from the eye, his function takes,
> The eare more quicke of apprehension makes.
> Wherein it doth impaire the seeing sense,
> It payes the hearing double recompence.
> Thou art not, by myne eye, Lysander, found:
> Mine eare, I thanke it, brought me to thy sound.

Pyramus' corresponding lines made us laugh at a shrewd perception turned into nonsense: "I see a voice: now will I to the chinke, / To spy and I can heare my Thisbyes face." The lines reminded Lysander of nothing.

Pyramus' and Thisby's protestations of fidelity underscored their insecure relationship to their world. Pyramus says, "Like Limander, am I trusty still," and Thisby responds, "And I, like Helen, till the fates me kill." Since Bottom's *Limander* sounded something like *Lysander*, "trusty as Lysander" suggested a premonitory truth about Pyramus: Lysander has abandoned Hermia for Helena in the wood, and Pyramus will fail to meet Thisby. Lysander noticed neither this parallel nor his own resemblance to an ancient hero.

"Like Limander" and "like Helen" carried our memories to the Homeric darlings of golden Aphrodite. *Limander*, when coupled with *Helen*, suggested *Alexander* (Greek *Alexandros*) by way of the corrupted form *Alisander*, naming the prince whom you often call *Paris*.[3] When we understood Pyramus to be claiming he is trusty "like Alexander," as well as almost saying "like Lysander," his oath sounded doubly funny, for we remembered that the false Trojan abandons Oenone for Helen, bringing Helen and ruin to his own city, and that after Menelaos has reclaimed Helen, he tries to reclaim Oenone. Thisby's "I, like Helen" sounded like an equally crippled oath of fidelity, of course, for we remembered the fabled Helen learning in whatsoever arms she is, therewith to be content—including, in recent memory, Doctor Faustus' arms.

We found the Babylonians' allusions to Cephalus and Procris more dreadfully malappropriate. Pyramus says, "Not Shafalus, to Procrus, was so true." And Thisby responds, "As Shafalus to Procrus, I to you." In the story known to readers of Ovid, the goddess Aurora falls in love with Cephalus, and when Cephalus will not forget his wife Procris, vengefully makes first faithfully loving Cephalus and then faithfully loving Procris jealous, and contrives that Cephalus must unintentionally and unknowingly kill Procris.[4]

Pyramus and Thisby, in their twisted and self-defeating declarations, invoking broken memories of unmanning sensuality, infidelity, unjustified jealousy, and unintended homicides, should have reminded Lysander, so we thought, of Hermia's elaborate oath to meet him outside the city. Hermia's pronunciation is better, but her invoked endorsers are equally bankrupt:

> I sweare to thee, by Cupids strongest bowe,
> By his best arrowe, with the golden heade,
> By the simplicitie of Venus doves,
> By that which knitteth soules, and prospers loves,
> And by that fire, which burnd the Carthage queene,
> When the false Trojan under saile was seene,
> By all the vowes that ever men have broke,
> (In number more then ever women spoke)
> In that same place thou hast appointed mee,
> To morrow truely will I meete with thee.

Cupid and Venus are rightly (and up to a point without irony) associated with "that which knitteth soules, and prospers loves," but as readers of Ovid also knew, they are whimsical. They produce confusion as blithely as Robin Goodfellow with the eyedrops. The fire that burned Dido (who had been touched by Cupid's arrow, so Virgil and Marlowe record) and the vows that men have broke provide questionable anchorage for an oath. The fact that Hermia fulfills her promise and meets Lysander told us—but of course not Lysander—that in Oberon's world a woman could keep her promise.

Seeing "Pyramus and Thisby" and remembering Lysander's naturalist assumptions about himself and his own world, we felt we beheld in Babylon a world these assumptions fit well enough for burlesque. We saw Wall behave like a wall, Moonshine like moonshine, Night like night, Lion like a lion, Pyramus like human Pyramus, and Thisby like human Thisby. Since no man, beast, or thing is connected with any principle capable of sustaining a relationship of any kind between men, beasts, and things, each acts only according to the law of his own being. Lysander of Athens sees the same world we see but does not guess that in his Athens, where Oberon's sporadically predestinating juices function, there is hope for love, passion can be reasonable, a covenant is sometimes dependable, and true lovers are not in every instance and circumstance crossed.

Northrop Frye in "The Argument of Comedy" says that comedy is designed "not to condemn evil but to ridicule the lack of self knowledge."[5] You may so regard *A Midsummer Night's Dream*. But we who went to church and read the Bible as diligently as we read Plato looked at man's ignorance, sometimes, from a slightly different angle. We recognized two ways of phrasing the knowledge that might lead to secular wisdom. The strong current of the Greek tradition where Frye still gracefully swims moved many to say (in Latin, of course) *nosce teipsum*, know yourself. Many in the Christian tradition thought that if the fear of the Lord is the beginning of wisdom the true route thereafter is the study of the wisdom of God as revealed in the Creation. Most of my friends subscribed to the value of both kinds of knowledge, but we found the play's unifying laughter directed toward an ignorance shared by Lysander and Pyramus, a misreading of the Book of Nature.

VIII

THE CITY MAN

> "Ay," quoth Jaques,
> "Sweep on, you fat and greasy citizens.
> 'Tis just the fashion. Wherefore do you look
> Upon that poor and broken bankrupt there?"
> Thus most invectively he pierceth through
> The body of the country, city, court.
> —*As You Like It*, II, i

THE MOST remarkable members of the English naturalist community, London citizens, would have angrily resented being called "Athenians," in ordinary circumstances. But in their jealous proprietorship over their town and their official hostility to unconventional talk they resembled the men who sentenced Socrates, and in their ways of posing and solving problems they resembled Greeks like Archimedes.

A Midsummer Night's Dream responded to recognition of the resemblance but did not demand it, for Bottom is more Elizabethan than Periclean. From the time workmen with English names, English jobs, and English jokes first appeared on stage, we heard modest but clear confirmations that London attitudes, traits, objects of attention, valuations, and assumptions were useful contexts to hold in our minds' antechambers. Whatever the status of craftsmen in legendary Athens or any other Mediterranean Athens, the craftsmen who offer to entertain Shakespeare's Theseus, hoping for a pension, were as normally English as Chaucer and his empty purse. Little as their "Pyramus and Thisby" looked like a great biblical play, its lines sounded less like Aristophanes than like an English citizen's effort. That was ironic in 1595 because, despite ceremonial shows at once honoring the queen and reiterating the companies' dignities, everybody knew that for more than twenty years the London city fathers had been attempting to have all plays stop together. To us all, Bottom—bumptious, energetic, ambitious, eager to do everything, quick as a tyrant to take charge, crude in his musical and literary tastes, concerned about etiquette in ladies' presence but unacquainted with courtly niceties, alternating between solicitude for his betters and a readiness to set them straight—outrageously imitated the English city man, whom Thomas Dekker's Shoemaker more straightforwardly presents.

Everybody in Shakespeare's first audiences well knew

that a picture representing city men as humble, ignorant, incurious, and undemanding tells less than half a truth. Quince introduces his actors not humbly, not defensively, but with pride: "Here is the scrowle of every mans name, which is thought fit, through al Athens, to play in our Enterlude, before the Duke, & the Dutches, on his wedding day at night." But the traits that these players exaggerated into caricature lent their antics a joy of recognition because the traits belonged to citizens functioning with confidence and purpose near a court that took for granted its social and intellectual superiority.

The more accurate and readily accessible your memories of the men who gave Bottom a living context in 1595 the more richly you may perceive in his dealings with Titania and "Pyramus and Thisby" a reflection of their practical self-confidence and philosophic obtuseness. Those laugh happily, to be sure, who laugh with the multitude, understanding Bottom as a stage bumpkin. If he reminds you of some loudmouthed small master weaver of your acquaintance, you laugh better. If you like Bottom and recognize in him traits you have noticed in great merchants, financiers, inventors, Francis Drakes, mining magnates, and manufacturers, you begin to laugh best of all.[1]

English culture has not preserved and transmitted an adequate memory of citizens and the city life known vividly to every playgoer who walked or rode out Bishopsgate Street to the Theater or Curtain. Aristocratic traditions and books calculated to make the heart race have so well preserved the lineaments of Sir Walter Ralegh, the Earl of Essex, and their peers[2] that when Touchstone in *As You Like It* loftily explicates rules of court etiquette and when Jacques catches him indulging the deep contemplative mood, everybody in the twentieth century can still perceive that the sophisticated clown mocks the well-educated courtier. English city men of great power, like Sir Thomas Gresham, William Hewett, Edward Osborne, and John Spencer, whom I personally knew or had known, are hardly more than names to you. Yet they, as well as humbler citizens, stand behind Bottom much as Sir Walter and my Lord of Essex stand behind Touchstone. The London citizen's twentieth-century counterpart does not reverence him, caring less about history than he did. No popular books burnish his paradoxical complexity to a romantic luster, and Dick Whittington is a nursery tale. As he accumulated wealth the citizen bred children, but they did not always imitate his life in shop, guildhall, and exchange. Those who succeeded to his business often started, like him, with the tough self-discipline of the ambitious poor and swept on, as he had done, to command luxury and men as if economic power was their own unaided achievement, boasting, not weeping, when they discarded a segment of the past.

Tombs, official records, institutions, customs, and nonromantic books can furnish you a limping magic to conjure up dimensions of London citizens as we knew them. Although manners have changed, as have relations with workmen and titles, their relationship to knowledge and their exercise of power make them more like their twentieth-century counterparts than the sixteenth-century courtier is like any living man. Instead of joiners and weavers you have industrial managers. A great merchant's wife no longer scandalizes moralists when she dresses like a queen, nor does she quite so frequently scheme to cuddle in her grandmotherly arms the grandson of a noble lord. But the merchant himself then and now has often sought an immortality by founding a college. Our city man was not only fathering the twentieth-century technology in the slow womb of time. He was already launching his ventures on ships that made good use of the stars and the backstaff and quadrant. Much of what you may recognize in Bottom as belonging to yourselves —his working assumptions about the world, his ways of manipulating it, his unawareness of his world's fundamental forces and his utter assurance that they are on his side—belongs to you because the London city man in his reincarnations has conquered the human world.

In 1595 *Citizens* did not include paupers and masterless men, of course, nor clergymen, the queen's officers, nor gentlefolk and noblemen residing in London. The word designated, rather, enfranchised makers, handlers, and sellers of things, devisers of enterprises, and their financiers.[3] Nearly all belonged to one or another of the companies whose names harked back to an earlier economic era (which for all I know may actually have existed) when every weaver spent most of his days tending a loom, every tailor sat from dawn to dusk making garments with his hands, every joiner had the smell of freshly planed wood always in his nostrils. But men's titles no longer so simply designated their daily tasks.

In sixteenth-century London, driving toward its destiny, the law-stiffened company boundaries rigidly limited no vigorous citizen's enterprise. Watchmakers (for social purposes often associated with the blacksmiths) prospered for years without a company of their own. A man proud to belong to the Mercers Company might do business as vintner or financier. A member of the Weavers Company, to be sure, was more likely than not to engage in England's major business of cloth and clothing, but a man whose title called him a loom operator might be a master, an employer, a buyer, and a seller. He might also make profits dealing wholesale in wheat, or like semifictional Simon Eyre, he might participate in large ventures overseas.

Philostrate describes the presenters of *Pyramus* as "Hard handed men, that worke in Athens here, / Which never labour'd in their minds till now." Granted, some in London who answered to "weaver" and "tinker" were dull workmen. Granted, your critics have followed William Hazlitt, who in *Characters of Shakespeare's Plays* accepts Quince and his friends at Philostrate's valuation without a qualm: "Bottom the Weaver . . . follows a sedentary trade, and he is accordingly represented as conceited, serious, and fantastical."[4] Even so you need not wholly follow Philostrate, whose very name suggests a passion for emphasizing class distinctions and who exemplifies the blinding snobbery that afflicted some Elizabethan gentlefolk. In their eyes all wealthy citizens were fat, greasy, deficient in sensitivity and in the manners you call urbane. They said "hempen homespunnes" and "rude mechanicals." Other gentlefolk knew better.

When George Unwin, author of *Industrial Organization in the Sixteenth and Seventeenth Centuries* (1904), sought to characterize earlier economic societies, he knew his readers would remember Chaucer and Shakespeare: "In every manufacturing town, craftsmen, who preserve the industrial type of Chaucer's day, and small masters, whose status resembles that of Shakespeare's Bottom the Weaver, are to be found in considerable numbers side by side with factory workers of the modern type."[5] In 1904 as later, small masters were not, as Unwin says, "obtruded upon the public notice." Small and large masters were decidedly obtruded upon the public notice in 1595.

Unwin's book stresses Elizabethan social and economic mobility, and you may verify his truth in histories of craft guilds and in biographies of families launched into greatness by successful merchants. Craftsman became master; small master became great master and small merchant; small merchant became great merchant; and master or merchant became, in impressive if rudimentary form, capitalist—all without losing his craft designation.[6]

Progress from apprenticeship to the rank of lord mayor or greater honors depended in part, to be sure, upon connections, skill in investing money, and the chances of economic life. But it also depended upon personal disposition, energy, and ambition. The success stories often sound like Horatio Alger. For instance when the infant daughter of Clothworker Sir William Hewett (lord mayor in 1559) fell into the Thames from London Bridge, she was rescued by an apprentice, Edward Osborne, destined to marry the girl, become Sir Edward and lord mayor, and sire a noble family.[7]

Although company membership distinguished one citizen from another, the really dramatic distinction set a boundary between the citizen of any kind and the courtier, especially such a courtier as might, like Lysander and Demetrius, be called "lord" without strain. Individuals like my father might be elevated, but most citizens as well as lords, in fiction and in actuality, loudly insisted on the dividing line. In Dekker's *Shoemakers' Holiday* a nobleman's son cannot peaceably love his Rose because she is daughter to a wealthy citizen. Clothworker Sir John Spencer, who became lord mayor the year before *A Midsummer Night's*

Dream was produced, was in temperament a prototype of Hermia's father and Thisby's. Sir John had a daughter, in love with young Lord Compton. When he attempted to play a role like Egeus, Lord Compton had him imprisoned for playing the parental tyrant. After an elopment the father eventually relented and accepted his son-in-law.[8] I suspect that Lady Spencer had an influence in these transactions.

All over England in 1595 merchants, manufacturers, entrepreneurs, bankers, shipowners, and tradesmen, employing an expanded political power, were giving cities a more and more taut control over English economic life.[9] Men apprenticed in cities other than London moved with equal confidence in the metropolis. Living prototypes of fictional Bottom and Quince, that is to say, included ship captains John Hawkins from Plymouth and his Devonshire kinsman Francis Drake.

Sea power was already escorting the bottoms of the city man's empire around the globe.[10] People in many ports were beginning to sweat to master our tongue, some to curse the English, like Caliban, but most to put shillings in their pockets. Wherever the English language went men would learn to think like English city men or remain forever "natives." In England the queen administered citizens' policies, and the nobility and gentry tried to evade their disciplining laws. Citizens were weaving the fabric of a new worldwide civilization, and insofar as foresight is possible, they knew it.

To a few playgoers, bitterly disposed, snobbish, or otherwise shortsighted, the rude mechanicals appeared instruments for a satire dismissing citizens from sympathy. Not everybody liked citizens. In 1595, however, the Establishment offered other whipping boys. Courtier and citizen alike were expected to deplore witches and the Pope, deplore politicians who mimicking Machiavelli listed obedience to God low on their criteria for decision, deplore alchemists for interfering with God's plan for metals, deplore gardeners who played the pimp to flowers, and deplore usury for loosening man's identity with a piece of land.

Sturdy citizens were stirring only mild apprehension.[11] The unrestrained exercise of their distinctive capabilities, nearly four hundred years before their methods would threaten the human race, was matter for comedy. Not until after the century turned and Elizabeth died would audiences, ignoring citizens' vast charitable activities, say "right" when Sir Giles Overreach as businessman would show himself incapable of understanding motives other than money and power; would show himself apt to damage anybody he might touch, including his own daughter. In Shakespeare's comedy, to be sure, Bottom and his friends triumph over rival candidates for entertaining the duke, but their victory hurts nobody we have come to know. I wasted no sympathy on the Athenian eunuch, the dancers of a tipsy bacchanal, and those who wanted to present the mourning muses. The traits that Bottom exhibits called memories of actual citizens; but instead of prompting satirical laughter they invited us to laugh well at Bottom himself—he was that much alive in our eyes.

Bottom's varieties of ignorance, notably his uproarious ignorance of the classics, lent a special substance to laughter in 1595. He has never before heard of Pyramus. In his own person or as Pyramus he so mispronounces *Hercules, Phoebus, Ninus, Alexander, Cephalus*, and *Procris*, familiar names out of Graeco-Roman stories, that his blunders provoke a quicker laughter than corresponding mistakes made by Oberon and the gentle Athenians. When he tries for apt allusions he mixes them so blatantly that not even editors attempt to blame textual contamination or Shakespeare's lapses of memory. Bottom is unlearned in a way that caricatures the results of London citizens' normal education, which paralleled gentlefolk's education only in the earliest years.

II / Bottom and the Death of Learning

Although most citizens, trained as apprentices, lacked what university life could supply, hundreds were intellectually competent by any but the classicist's standard. Immensely curious, they devoured the translated lore of Rome, Athens, France, and dangerous Italy almost as avidly as the Englished Bible. To satisfy their passion for the facts and figures of their world, presses worked steadily, if with less than Italian precision. Their curiosity was not limited. Bottom, when he wanted to know the phase of the moon, was putting to normal use the kind of almanac that Leonard Digges and his son Thomas repeatedly issued. But almanacs were also manuals in astrology and natural history. It was for citizens that Thomas Digges' revised edition carried an abridged Copernicus.[12]

In the sixteenth century the words *learned* and *learning* carried a more specific meaning than in the twentieth. A learned man characteristically formed his thoughts to fit the intellectual paradigm of Christendom: truth is the living content of God's mind. Though part of that divine wisdom was to be sought in the mysteries of Nature, a scholar's first duty was to master the truth discerned by earlier scholars or recorded in Scripture. When he subsequently studied any natural thing in itself, he recognized that the part nearest the mind of God is its spirit or soul, and he remembered that all parts of Nature cohere in a grand unity. In reading afresh from Nature (his bodily senses being notoriously fallible since the Fall)[13] he would be particularly prudent with physical aspects. Only after testing a new finding by its congeniality with previously recorded truth would he commit it to writing.

Learning thus had a content and a process, but above all it had a language. A learned man might know Greek grammar, but by definition he knew Latin. From Latin texts we knew the substance of Herodotus and Thucidides, Homer and Virgil, Ovid and Plautus, Aristotle and Plato, Epicurus and Lucretius, Cicero and Seneca, Augustine and Aquinas, Boethius and Hippocrates, Ptolemy and Pliny. Whatever was serious in more recent thought we expected to find in Latin.[14]

If one did not know the things inevitably learned in elemen-tary Latin, he obviously did not know Latin. Men who rose to power in London through apprentice training, however much they might have acquired from English books, lacked Latin. Some of us sons of citizens studied Latin, as at the great Merchant Taylors School with Mulcaster, but many did not. Without Latin, citizens were not learned, and they knew it, though they had done more reading than any other unlearned people in England and were confident in their knowledge and skill. Bottom's blunders in Ovid's stories loudly confirmed that he had no Latin. It does not, of course, follow that we learned London citizens were exempt from belonging to the context in which Bottom stands.

Most London citizens admired conventional learning and evinced special enthusiasm for the learned man's model of the spiritually dominated world. They supposed that the existence of angels, devils, ghosts, witches, fairies, and themselves as primarily souls was clearly implied by Christian doctrine. Their laws about blasphemy, church attendance, and self-indulging pleasures they vocally justified less by business considerations than by asserting that man's chief end is to glorify God and that nothing carnal should divert the mind. They paid homage to the warm concept of a spirit-directed world whenever they deplored their lust, anger, frivolity, irreverence, and raw greed, and often when they responded to music, flowers, and the kindnesses of friends.

Their major instrument of self-discipline, hope, and gratitude, was prayer. They prayed at meals, on rising, at bed time, in court, in church, before and after battles, at a birth, at a wedding, at a death, and on making a contract.[15] They also made gestures of spiritual contact in less Christian contexts, so that it is not entirely unfair to call London citizens more superstitious than men who had attended the universities. When they heard Pyramus caricature the postulate of the organic world by speaking conversationally to everything he notices, they could not wholly say, "Not me."

The citizen paid tribute to learning when, as he often did, he sent his son to grammar school and then to Oxford or Cambridge. When a graduate returned to London his father had reason to expect that he might pursue not the making and distribution of goods but a learned profession or the service of a nobleman, church, or sovereign, though some of us would live mainly by our wits, like Ben Jonson.[16]

We graduates tended to agree with our mothers that learning made us superior to the apprentice-trained working citizen. In music we were apt to relish the lute song more and more, tongs and bones less and less; in poetry apt to relish the condoling sonnet and things like "Venus and Adonis" more, "Ercles vaine, a tyrant's vaine" less. However irksome our sophisticated tastes, such results did not dissuade other fathers from sending sons to grammar school and university. Learned men had a teaching function in society, whether in classroom, courtroom, church, or palace, and citizens seconded their precepts whenever these corroborated the moral world view and reinforced inducements to personal and civic virtue. Citizens felt betrayed when a learned man talked like an atheist, and in that fact resides an irony.

However ostentatiously their prayers, myths, laws, and self-discipline endorsed an organic world model ordered by love, however regularly their knees, reiterating the central paradigm, said Lord, Lord, and however eagerly their support of classical education testified to an exalted esteem for conventional learning, the powerful actions of London citizens were unbuilding the structure of the old world's kinship. In solving the intrinsic problems of their businesses they did not employ learned postulates. They were building a material world with parts as discrete as Democritus' atoms or English coins. Untroubled by the disparity, they produced on the stage of the world a grim comedy in which, considering the action, there was not one word apt. We half remembered that tragical human comedy as we held our sides and laughed at Bottom. Bottom is not Machiavellian but inept, not vindictive but clumsy, not cynical but hopeful. Bottom is nevertheless a monster, with and without his ass's head. Happily he is not loathsome but lovable.

Despite teachers with advanced sympathies like Mulcaster, the time had not yet come for giving the name *learning* to naturalist problem solving. A few years later Bacon's title *The Advancement of Learning* would sound revolutionary—as revolutionary as *Novum Organum*—when people saw what it meant. But as early as 1581 the instrument maker Robert Norman had praised the method whose direction Bacon was to follow. He proudly distinguished himself, an experimenter and "mechanician" content with English, from "the learned." In his address to the reader, prefaced to his book *The Newe Attractive*, he says:

I do verily think, that notwithstanding the learned . . . being in their studies amongst their books, can imagine great matters, and set down their far fetched conceits, in fair show and with plausible words, wishing that all mechanicians were such as for want of utterance should be forced to deliver unto them their knowledge and conceits, that they might flourish upon them, and apply them at their pleasures: yet there are in this land divers mechanicians that in their several faculties and professions have the use of those arts at their fingers ends, and can apply them to their several purposes as effectually and more readily than those that would most condemn them. For albeit they have not the use of the Greek and Latin tongues, to search the variety of authors in those arts, yet have they in English for geometry Euclid's elements, with absolute demonstrations: and for arithmetic Record's works, both his first and second part: and divers others, both in English and in other vulgar languages, that have also written of them, which books are sufficient to the industrious mechanician, to make him perfect and ready in those sciences, but especially to apply the same to the art or faculty which he chiefly professeth.[17]

With prophetic souls we who loved the art, logic, and morals of the learned world watched its power decline as citizens, intellectually bold but untaught in traditional values, acquired power.

For a fleeting moment Philostrate reminded us of the loss, when he provides Theseus an opportunity to hear "The Thrise three Muses, mourning for the death / Of learning, late deceast in beggery." Naturalist Theseus, not given to breast-beating anyhow, declines: "That is some Satire keene and critical, / Not sorting with a nuptiall ceremony."

The sense of "death" in "death of learning" Friedrich Nietzsche and his followers made familiar when they proclaimed the "death of God."[18] Not everybody would agree with

Donne when fifteen or so years after the first showing of *A Midsummer Night's Dream* he lamented the death of the old philosophy.[19] In 1595, however, we could all understand a satirist reading an obituary. Nobody had killed learning, neither with bow
and arrow nor with corrosive criticism—though there was that
in plenty, directed particularly against Aristotle, the philosopher
beloved of clerks of Oxenford[20]—nor even with the industrial
machinery that was multiplying pounds sterling for the "unlearned." Learning in the old sense was suffering the first stages
of hypokinetic disease. Its model of the world, created in the
likeness and image of a whole man, was hardly more useful to
philosophers stoking the fires of the scientific revolution than to
citizens reaching for tools effective in the practice of their crafts.

The sensitive part of our souls, deft in the old ways, had
enough cause for apprehension when we began to think that our
dear England might come into the hands of men who did not
know a kingdom's basic anatomy and physiology. But something closer to the heart than governmental structure was en-
dangered. We saw the mechanicals creating with their skit an
absurd world model that better fits the craftsmen's unexamined
postulates than the saint's creed. Our mirth was faintly tragical,
for our bones muttered that the shadow falling athwart the
world wherein the painting of Giotto and the goodness of his
Saint Francis made sense was the shadow of comfortless death.
We had not ignored the old Duke of Norfolk when he said that
"England was never merry since the new learning came up."[21]

In none of his roles, however—paramour, actor, Pyramus—
did Bottom exemplify absurdities monopolized by citizens. I
have suggested our recognition that Lysander's counterparts in
England, building upon Archimedes, Galen, and the pre-Socratic
philosophers, were remaking the philosophical world with
words to fit men's minds for the material world the citizens
were remaking. And as often as citizens we gentle folk, impelled
by dawn and despair, knelt before the God of our fathers. We saw
in ourselves the citizen behavior which Bottom mirrored. Contemplating that mirror, we laughed without much wincing, for

Bottom invited us both to know ourselves and to sustain for ourselves a real affection.

No lethargy of mind characterized London citizens in 1595. In shop and exchange, on land and sea, in political manipulation and in wrestling with time, materials, and physical forces they went about their chores in Robert Norman's unlearned but successful way. They did not bother to phrase an alternative model of the world: they proceeded, logic be hanged, without any such concept at all. The working weaver, for example, practicing an efficient and complex craft, could deal with most factors— sources of thread, markets, space for equipment, treatment of apprentices, and so on—according to mere custom. In contriving those new devices of production which his company's regulations urged upon him, his procedures were naturalist and concentrated on the problem at hand. When he wanted a new design in cloth he modified the arrangement of the loom. He might retain an old bit of structure out of mere muscular habit, but he did not, like the great woodcarvers, worship God with his tools. He owed diligence to God. He owed a reliable product to a customer. He owed an efficient invention to his company and himself.

III / Citizens and the Conquest of Nature

In his shop he followed a scheme of action that would later be used in industrial research laboratories: he contrived models till he found one that gave an economical solution to his problem, rejecting those that did not work so well. His procedures resembled Bacon's experiments, which had their exclusions of negative instances as well as their affirmations.[22] The improvements he made in his inventions (though they were sometimes in effect extensions of his hands and similarly obeyed his eye) reduced more and more the sense that they had an organic connection with his hand.[23]

In contrast with early heroes of modern science like William Gilbert shaping his spherical magnet, craftsmen escaped the compulsion to fit the solutions of their problems into the metaphysical design of the universe. Clockmakers might have been tempted. De'Dondi in fourteenth-century Italy made a device that was both clock and planetarium, and the great Strasbourg Cathedral clocks illustrate how many recurring events early clockmakers sought to bring under prediction.[24] The proliferation of automata so characteristic of late twentieth-century life and instruments of death had started in 1595. By linking a timing mechanism to other mechanisms to produce the motions of human acts, clockmakers were already teasing the imagination.[25] Clocks themselves, like human beings, have always been designed to run in harmony with celestial events such as the progress of each day. After a few years philosophers would take the clock for an apt model of God's creation. However, though automata from the days of ancient Egypt have often been used in rituals, they are obviously physical things, using physical forces and duplicating physical events. Our clockmakers felt no more mystical than pump makers, gunsmiths, compass makers, and other manufacturers of things that move or cause movement without animal pressures.

Craftsmen's inventions, when learned men noticed them, produced intellectual stresses that demanded a more and more finite mode of thought. William Gilbert's fame among scientists, who seldom praise him for his words about souls, rests as much on his naturalist attitude towards evidence—for which he was partly indebted to citizen Robert Norman's *Newe Attractive*—as on his substantive statements, some of which Norman anticipated. When John Davis invented the backstaff and quadrant he gave new firmness to astronomers' thinking. Craftsmen whose pumps sucked water out of coal mines and those whose cannon put balls into trajectories exerted pressures on budding physicists. And clockmakers, dividing time into manageable segments, facilitated scientific descriptions of events.

As the passage quoted from Robert Norman suggests, the learned often quizzed "mechanicians" about their procedures and filched "knowledge and conceits"—or accepted what was acceptable—for their books. Craftsmen mainly wanted to make things, but many liked to describe their methods. Norman spoke for many a craftsman curious about the properties of his materials and bent on understanding any recurring event he could put to use. He was not apt to talk about the great scheme of things or Aristotle but rather what his own active hands had taught him. Juan Vives, who visited England more than half a century before 1595, had recommended that philosophers observe artisans, and so had Rabelais.[26] Francis Bacon had not yet outlined his proposal for a history of trades, but he was already impressed by observant habits in men whose livelihood depended upon devising and handling machines, instruments, and tools.[27]

Craftsmen were not the only citizens who fostered a naturalist approach to the world. Sir Thomas Gresham, whom my father admired, exemplified Londoners' emphasis in education. Member of the powerful Mercers Company, extraordinary economic adviser and loyal servant to a grateful queen, manipulator, founder of the Royal Exchange, not necessarily the most scrupulous man in England but the richest, he bequeathed London a dream and a promise. At his death in 1579 he left a will stipulating that his great London house, after his wife's death, should become the home of Gresham College. Seven professors, unmarried (shades of *Love's Labour's Lost!*), should give free lectures on divinity, astronomy, law, music, geometry, medicine, and rhetoric. Although the list does not sound like the curriculum of a modern institute of technology, its distinctive emphasis pressed the mathematical study of nature. Lady Gresham did not wither out all the young college's revenue, though eighteen years elapsed before she made way. Before the end of 1597 the Mercers trustees had appointed and installed the professors, and the lectures had begun.[28]

When *A Midsummer Night's Dream* began playing, its audiences could not know how remarkably Gresham College would serve as a gathering place for scientific folk or foresee its role in the founding of the Royal Society.[29] But we knew the recommendations and stipulations in Gresham's will. As Foster Watson has noted, Gresham urged the lecturers to "remember that the hearers of the lectures would be 'merchants and other citi-

zens,' and therefore he says the lectures are not to be 'read after
the manner of the Universities, but let the reader cull out such
heads of his subject as may best serve the good liking and capacity of the said auditory.'"

The astronomy professor was to read "the principles of the sphere and
the theoriques of the planets, and to explain the use of common instruments for the capacity of mariners," and was to apply "these
things" to use by reading geography, and the art of navigation. The
geometry professor was to lecture for one term on arithmetic; the next
on theoretical geometry; and the third on practical geometry. In music
"the lecture was to be read, the theoretic part for one half-hour or
thereabouts, and the practical part by help of voices or instruments for
the rest of the hour." It will thus be seen that Sir Thomas Gresham
brought into useful study modern subjects not then taught in
Grammar Schools, and but little in the Universities, that he encouraged practical methods to be used, and that he required the subjects to
be taught in English and not in Latin.[30]

The plan for Gresham College laid the ground for our understanding of a major component of *A Midsummer Night's
Dream*. The college answered the aspirations of people who instead of wondering about strange phenomena used them to
achieve power and control, who regarded the angelic human
mind as a device for turning a profit. Memories of these vigorous
men and women, brought to the level of easy recognition by Sir
Thomas Gresham's great benefaction, helped to give a substantial meaning to the soulless Babylonian world which Bottom
and his citizen colleagues tinkered into existence for Pyramus
and Thisby. But best of all, we found the Babylonian world intelligible because we had come to know Citizen Bottom and to
appreciate his incapability to comprehend the glorious episode
which he called his dream.

IV / Bottom
and the
Spiritual
Understanding
of the World

Reflective men laughed along with giggling girls at Bully Bottom, ass head and all, issuing orders that fall short of exercising
the attentive fairies' full panoply of marvelous capabilities. We
laughed in the same company when we saw him fail to exploit
the fairy queen's ultimate offers. But as we laughed like sopho-
mores we enjoyed philosophic amusement too.

As we watched Bottom we remembered citizens whose minds raucously demanded to know Nature and whose bold hands itched to control her—citizens scheming to turn Nature's forces to uses profitable for men's comfort, health, power, and joy. We also recognized that in the Athenian world of *A Midsummer Night's Dream* Titania, second only to Oberon—if indeed second—is the controlling goddess of Nature. In the delectable lap of this goddess, who holds answers to Nature's mysteries and whose personality controls its bounty, Citizen Bottom plops his bored head and snores away as if in church. He never asks Titania a single interesting question. With the best opportunity in his animated world to command Nature, he says, "Scratch my heade, Pease-blossome." This from the kind of man whose London prototype vehemently said *Amen* to the proposition that the important answers are spiritual answers! We thought of Doctor Faustus, who paid with his soul for powers freely offered to Bottom out of love. Faustus tragically fritters away his powers on trivia. Bottom fritters, but not tragically. He behaves like a naturalist who would not recognize the Queen of Nature if he saw her in a wood, let alone quiz her about astronomy, meteorology, hydraulics, cannon ball trajectories, and ways to spare London the plague.

Hearing Bottom's amazed paean when he wakes after his enchanted night, we remembered Saint Paul's words of promise: "Eye hath not seen, nor ear heard, neither have entered into the heart of man, the things which God hath prepared for them that love him." Bottom says, "The eye of man hath not heard, the eare of man hath not seene, mans hand is not able to taste, his tongue to conceive, nor his hearte to report, what my dreame was." Bottom's confusion of organs and senses is funny enough by itself, but it was funnier to those of us who recognized the twisted quotation in its Pauline context. The whole of the eloquent second chapter of the First Epistle to the Corinthians contrasts the poor "wisdom of the world" with the "wisdom of God": the things knowable by the "natural man" (by naturalists, for instance) with "that which the Holy Ghost teacheth" (things knowable through communion of spirit). The very Queen of

Nature and its mysteries has answers to questions asked and not yet asked, has ready at her hand the gift of powers coveted and not yet coveted, all for a Bottom who might love her. Bottom flubs the opportunity. We might have wept.

But as we heard Bottom butchering a scripture which praises spiritual learning we did not cry. We had heard Puritan citizens quote the passage at the very time they were flouting it, and that was tragic. Bottom was not tragic. We laughed till tears cleansed our eyes.

IX THE INDUCTIVE PATTERN AND SIXTEENTH-CENTURY HABITS OF ATTENTION

When I have seen by Time's fell hand defaced
The rich proud cost of outworn buried age;
When sometime lofty towers I see down-rased,
And brass eternal slave to mortal rage;
When I have seen the hungry ocean gain
Advantage on the kingdom of the shore,
And the firm soil win of the wat'ry main,
Increasing store with loss and loss with store;
When I have seen such interchange of state,
Or state itself confounded to decay;
Ruin hath taught me thus to ruminate
That Time will come and take my love away.

—Sonnet 64

W E WERE prepared by many instances, some far from science, to recognize and relish the inductive pattern of reasoning with which we were ourselves further preparing the English mind to sustain superstructures of the later world. Those of us who had read Shakespeare's sixty-fourth sonnet had recognized the pattern in the mutability quatrains: data accumulated from diverse situations that involve change, the lover's generalizing affirmation, and the divination of a particular event in the lover's future. We also knew that a prince, an investing merchant, or a politician—even if his interest led him to observe the same phenomena—would be likely to predict a different future event. We were ready for *A Midsummer Night's Dream*—which reinforced our tendency to perceive and use inductive sequences by rewarding it with food for laughter. In an age that took rhetoric seriously we were accustomed to notice these and other verbal organizations. We had a context for amusement at characters who employ obtrusive schemes like anaphora and zeugma, who imitate Lyly's mannerisms, or who ape the solecisms of men with no Ciceronian experience; but we found a particular pleasure in characters who exhibit for comedy the brave new patterns of man thinking.

Our verbal habits differed from yours, in a way. Speakers and hearers in any age commonly leave unexamined most designs in their speech, noticing only what is uncommon or brought to focus by contrast or some other device. You are liable to give disproportionate weight to commonplace sixteenth-century locutions, liable to take a secular passage as consciously or deeply religious because of an unemphatic "God willing." Unless you look carefully, statements in naturalist form by men like Dee and Ralegh and characters like Lysander and Theseus—evidence of daring minds when framed—may escape you because they conform to paradigms that come to you as second nature because inherited from the likes of them and me. You are beneficiaries of advanced thinkers in 1595 who shook the bars of the syllogism, and went a new way. For mild pains, however, you can partly dismantle what we did to the language and recapture the capacity for fresh recognition that people like us brought to *A Midsummer Night's Dream*.

Basically as old as trial and error and seldom noticed in many familiar situations, inductive procedures were being put to formal use in contexts previously reserved for authoritative utterances. Though Heisenberg[1] and electronic astronomers[2] had not made their pronouncements, advanced thinkers still knew from tradition that some questions about nature's behavior were unanswerable in natural terms. But their naturalist procedures were beginning to shake that knowledge, beginning to persuade us all to assume an absolute infallibility in nature. We were ever more and more disposed to attribute to human limitations our failures to achieve perfect predictions. Aware, therefore, that every step in our characteristic sequence (data, general proposition, testing) could be a misstep, and not yet quite confident in the whole procedure, we were ready to find our mode of inquiry fit for comic scrutiny.

Before I ask you to join me for a final look at the inductive structures I saw in *A Midsummer Night's Dream* I want to describe some of the ways in which we were acquiring inductive habits of mind. When I draw on drama itself for illustration I shall use plays very familiar to you, including some that appeared after 1595.

II /
Popularization
of Inductive
Habits

The thinking that led to Newtonian physics depended in part upon a capability honored before Plato and signally honored in our time, the capability to perceive resemblances among differing things and events. Both religious and naturalist thinkers exploited resemblances. The one sought a place for the natural datum in the total rhythmic ordering of the world's immense chaos—in the mind of God. The other sought a place for the natural datum in a context of other data demonstrably associated with it.

Both religious and naturalist patterns of reasonableness often occurred in the discourse of a single writer or a single character in a play. When Portia is laying her trap for Shylock, she claims for mercy that "It is an attribute to God himself; / And earthly power doth then show likest God's / When mercy seasons justice" (*Merchant of Venice*, IV, i, 195–97). But when, approaching Belmont by night, she is relishing the music that sounds from her house and finds it sweeter than she remembers it by day, she speculates to Nerissa,

> The crow doth sing as sweetly as the lark
> When neither is attended, and I think
> The nightingale, if she should sing by day,
> When every goose is cackling, would be thought
> No better a musician than the wren.
> How many things by season season'd are
> To their right praise and true perfection!
> (*Merchant of Venice*, V, i, 102–106)

In both sequences Portia perceives resemblances and shows a predilection for due proportion. But she looks at data differently and reaches her end by two different routes. She moralizes to Shylock like an old-fashioned Christian or Hebrew, testing human behavior by its congruence with a divine original. But when for the aesthetic problem she devises a naturalist model, her argument satisfies by recording phenomena that exhibit a common pattern. Then she ventures a prediction in a quasiexperimental situation and concludes by announcing a general proposition all of whose components are finite.

I must not exaggerate the degree to which the second sequence exemplifies later thought. What Portia says is not perilous; it threatens no article of faith. She does not illustrate the matured skepticism, precision, and passion for quantification and foresight that has graced the great mathematical physicists. Alfred North Whitehead's statement shows their more specific emphasis. The inductive function for scientists, he says, is "not

. . . in its essence the derivation of general laws." It is rather "the divination of a particular future from the known characteristics of a particular past."[3] The kind of understanding Portia aims at here nevertheless appealed to us who admired Francis Bacon.

Bacon's 1605 proclamation of the inductive method has great merits, but it did not offer all the novelty some have claimed for it. He phrases beautifully a procedure already practiced in 1595. An investigator using the method, he says, tries first to isolate what is common to a group of natural events and then lists all available instances in which the common something (the "nature") is present. He considers, then rejects, instances which at first glance appeal for inclusion but upon examination are found to lack the "nature." He ventures an affirmation or general statement and measures its validity against the included instances. He refines his affirmation and tests it again, more rigorously, wherever possible using an experiment, which is a derived instance designed to compel a segment of nature to provide an answer to a specific question.[4]

Robert Norman, years earlier, used data in the way Bacon advocated. Describing the behavior of the loadstone and the compass needle, Norman appeals to evidence provided by repeated experiments. He asks questions in an inductive way. In his brief prefatory remarks in *The Newe Attractive* he says:

And as I may not, nor mean herein willingly to condemn the learned or ancient writers, that have with great diligence labored to discover the secrets of Nature in sundry things, with their operations and causes, yet I mean God willing, without derogating from them, or exalting myself, to set down a late experimented truth found in this stone, contrary to the opinions of all them that have heretofore written thereof. Wherein I mean not to use barely, tedious conjectures or imaginations, but briefly as I may, to pass it over, founding my arguments only upon experience, reason, and demonstration, which are the grounds of Arts.

Ordinary events stood ready to reinforce inductive thought. Individual experience kept her dear school. Children learned to dread fire, youths learned to pursue particular young women, and women learned to thread needles—each by arraying in memory a cluster of related data in recognizable, repeatable situations. Even before they had become philosophers, natural philosophers had thus learned to recognize the structures of situations, impelled by a hope to exercise control.

Like the ancient Greeks and the author of the Book of Ecclesiastes, sixteenth-century men noted nature's great cycles, but we carried our appetite for repetitions much farther. We found them in the musical canon and fugue, in identical twins, in alliterations and assonances, in the quibble (anathema, even before Dr. Johnson, to people devoted to simple precision), in the rebus, the allegory, the common law, syntactical repetitions like anaphora, and rimes like *womb* and *tomb* which by playing upon mere echoes tease the mind into alertness for thematic relationships and new unities. We recognized a more-than-superficial resemblance among cross, cathedral, sword, and flying bird, among the spherical shapes of solar system, earth, and Gilbert's magnets, among structures of authority in family, city, kingdom, church, and universe.

Whenever we perceived resemblances, we played a witty game that exercised our social imaginations for the new mode of understanding. The community of imaginations thus in training needed only discipline—and a command of mathematics—to fit it for the scientific revolution, needed only Shakespeare to afford us insights at *A Midsummer Night's Dream*, *King Lear*, and *The Tempest*.

III / The Drama and Inductive Reasoning

Our taste for patterns in nature and society made us look for patterns in the drama. Dr. John Dee noticed that water would not fall to a surrounding level when it filled a container partly submerged, open end down, in water—or rise to a surrounding level when an empty container was thrust, open end down, deep into water. Dee did not invent the barometer or phrase Boyle's law, but as he asked what factor makes water reach its level in one situation and not in another, he was learning how to ask questions of nature. When a playgoer who had learned to ask such a question noticed two stories of eloping lovers and noticed that one story ends happily, the other dreadfully, he was apt to ask what factor makes the difference. If he asked at *A Midsummer Night's Dream* he found an answer.

As you watch Elizabethan plays invite inductive responses to dramatic structures you may find yourselves tempted into a speculation: how far was the theater responsible for sharpening habits of attention that undergirded the scientific revolution, how far responsible for preparing men to welcome the great physicists when they came? But of course I thought of no such questions, and our business together leads us a more fruitful way. I shall describe habits that prepared English minds to exercise themselves inductively, and if inductively then joyously, at *A Midsummer Night's Dream*.

Many plays lay no demands upon any intellectual capability worth the name, offer no invitation to any new perception. Plautus rings undemanding changes on unsurprising themes, as does your classic Western movie. Plautus has his charm and *High Noon* is superb because every moment, with a persuasiveness like a ritual or the rising sun, contributes to a known, loved cliché.

Many plays that make authentic demands give exercise to capabilities other than the inductive. They appeal to honorable forms of curiosity kept in health by Virgil, Dante, the exemplum, and mathematical systems. Such were many early didactic plays in England. Whenever chorus or prologue "cannot keep counsel" but tells all at the outset, the audience's inductive capability sleeps. The World's Ultimate Authority begins the Norwich play of "The Creation of Eve and the Fall"[5] with an announcement which the other characters then translate into action. At the beginning of Bale's play, King John announces a royal purpose, and then event after event expresses it.

In the Greek tragedies events are, to be sure, so deployed that if Athenians had not already been informed they would have come inductively to perceive Clytemnestra's character, for example, or to grasp earlier than Hippolytus the particular fate that will destroy him. But each play's central action leads to a grand tragic awareness not so much by inviting playgoers to derive from data an unprecedented understanding as by persuading them that, as in Euclid, the end is a true end of the beginning. The initial narrative situation persuasively necessitates the next, and so on through a series of *therefore*'s to the last event, which answers the necessity set up at the beginning. E. M. Forster in *Aspects of the Novel* calls such a plot superior to mere story because the constitutents are bound together by cause. The causal tradition has not dominated all great fictions. Nowadays, when it does prevail in movie, novel, or play, it seems to provide you a reassuring, old-fashioned comfort. An alternative mode tends to stimulate inductive thought. As non-Euclidean as seven-dimensional polytopes, it is no twentieth-century invention.

William Empson and after him Richard Levin have called to your attention ways in which the double plot appealed to audiences in my lifetime and earlier. "Much can be put into it," says Empson; "to those who miss the connections the thing still seems sensible, and queer connections can be insinuated powerfully and unobtrusively; especially if they fit in with ideas the audience already has at the back of its mind." The good Elizabethan audience, in addition to preconceived ideas, brought to drama a sharpened capability (recaptured by Empson) to respond to what Levin calls "analogical . . . relationships . . . between plots."[6]

But the inductive capability was exercised not only by responses to analogous plots. By noticing resemblances among events, characters, settings, phrases, or whatever else was partially repeated, philosophic thinkers had a particularly good time at some plays. If one event occurred, it was simply an event. But if after a while another event caught the attention, not because it was caused by the first but because it resembled it in some interesting way, we remembered the two events together and felt a unity. We felt a special satisfaction if looking about within a play we found that each resembling factor con-

fers meaning on each other factor, and all of them collectively
on each, and each on the whole. We enjoyed an organic play in
an organic world.

By responding to some mystery plays in this fashion, even as
we submitted to their demand for reverent contemplation of
God's compassionate mind, we put our imaginations to school.
At the Brome play of Abraham and Isaac those who saw it
noticed that Isaac's obedience to Abraham resembles Abraham's
obedience to God. Whatever may have been their opinion of the
doctrine, they felt horror at Abraham's intention and an awareness of his agony as he prepares to sacrifice his son. But at the
moment when Abraham is about to kill, Isaac's submission so
recalled Jesus' submission to God in Gethsemane that Abraham's agony also dramatized for them God's anguish in sac-
rificing the Christ. They did not simply climb on Abraham's
pain to witness the depth of God's concern for their salvation.
Abraham's pain remained in clear focus, emphasizing and being
emphasized by God's.

Though Isaac was traditionally associated with the Lamb of
God and certain words in the dialogue—"blyssyd body" and "Let
it passe over"—recalled ritual passages, the religious statement
heavily relied on audience alertness to perceive a dramatized incident in the remembered context of another incident. The inductive capability enabled the audience to divine that Abraham's anguish, less generous than God's, is still Godlike, even
though they did not see God as actor. The Brome play, which
thus exploits the Christian's training to interpret an incident in
the Old Testament as a prefiguration of an incident in the New
and to proceed from earthly occurrences to contemplation of
heavenly, demanded only an easy step beyond the familiar skills
of homiletic interpretation. It illustrates the evolution of a new
species of thought out of established modes, and it exemplifies
the writers' contribution to that development.

The unforgettable *Second Shepherds Play* depended upon the
existence of minds thus trained. By paralleling the story of thiev-
ing Mak and his cradled sheep with the familiar event in Beth-
lehem, the Wakefield Master demanded of his fellow citizens

that they either dismiss the play as a hodgepodge or achieve in their hearts a complex fresh understanding of God's wonderful ways.

At plays of later years we noticed similar bold juxtapositions of two stories. Each story line proceeded as traditionally or as casually as you please, but when as a coupled pair they provided parallel sequences for nonsibling sons or for two kinds of babies, or when they showed two pairs of lovers, two fathers, two kinds of national glorification, two kinds of magic, or two kinds of womanly triumph, the whole play invited our minds to behold clusters of data thus brought into focus—invited us to understandings inductively achieved. We accepted the invitation.

The double story afforded inductive exercise throughout the great dramatic flowering, especially but not exclusively in Shakespeare. We followed Bianca's love story and Katherine's in *The Taming of the Shrew*, Hero's and Beatrice's in *Much Ado About Nothing*, and the story of Gloucester paralleling the story of Lear. But we also found England's glory exemplified in one way by Bacon and another way by Margaret in Greene's *Friar Bacon and Friar Bungay*. We saw a tragic misuse of power and a farcical misuse in Marlowe's *Doctor Faustus*. The winning of Rose and the redemption of Jane commented on one another in Dekker's *Shoemakers' Holiday*.

Our predisposition led us to notice instances when characters themselves exercise—or conspicuously fail to exercise—inductive thought. Such characters do people the plays. So do characters who manipulate other characters by conducting pseudo-experiments—devised incidents wherein an outcome more or less honestly tests a prediction. Thus Poins invites Hal to join in the Gadshill robbery, predicting that Falstaff will run away and then lie about it. We saw Falstaff imitating the generosity of nature when he makes his lies unexpectedly and comprehensively informative. Hamlet claims success for his "Mousetrap" experiment, though he imitates a conscientious, objective experimenter abominably, bellowing at the king at the crucial moment. Iago devises a villainous false laboratory demonstration, inducing Othello to swallow the inference that

Cassio's predicted gestures confirm carnal familiarity with Desdemona. Such "experiments" do their dramatic work partly because, as new philosophers sensed, they lack controls and do not address themselves to disinterested inquiries. But we also noted the dangerous propensity of human observers (which we knew we shared) to leap inductively to conclusions sharply at variance with the true evidence. Our interests led us beyond such set pieces to think about each play in its entirety. Often our examination of the anatomy of a dramatic action led us through an inductive sequence to infer laws operating in the world which the play brings into existence.

As compared with the fugue, the emblem, the metaphor, and such like structures of resemblance, the inductively patterned play, including the play with two stories, was a more reassuring training ground for the imagination. We accumulated material for a new concept, not as two or three factors triggered a single flash of recognition, but as the storing memory appealed for a progressively more satisfying formulation while event after event discharged its cargo of meaning. The inductively patterned play differed from the poetic allegory, which asks readers to recognize a second, more momentous sequence under the guise of the first. As we followed a play we looked at each component strand in the light of all the others, at mutual reinforcements and modifications through successive situations and events. The fresh concepts did not peep from behind events but put the events into a design that enriched them for the heart.

Comedies used the double story more often than tragedies, but the device shows its power in *King Lear*.[7] In this play we saw an inevitability as fearsome as in *Oedipus*. We contemplated with terror the consequences of headstrong behavior (Gloucester's blinding and death, Lear's madness and death) and shared the recognition that comes to each doomed father. But as we explored the two fathers' predicaments we called the dramatic world itself into question. When we urgently asked what put each father's tragic course in motion, we were also asking to what degree Lear's was ultimately a reliable world, whether its responses to human conduct suggested a tolerable hierarchy of moral laws. Contrasting events and circumstances common to the two families began to clarify some values, with negative as well as affirmative instances. Although Edmund is a bastard, Lear's children are all legitimate, so in Lear's world adultery is not the major sin. Since Gloucester's children are boys, Lear's girls, it is not the sex of a child that predisposes him to piety or villainy or stupid goodness. I for one associated Lear's folly with one kind of impatience, Gloucester's with another kind, and then Cordelia's and Edmund's and Goneril's with still other kinds. Was it possible that in the world of *Lear* impatience is a cardinal sin? The play provoked substantial inquiries that provided fewer answers than new questions.

As we watched *Lear* proceed through its complex situations and events and followed tragic characters as they acquire a somewhat clearer vision, we sifted, discarded, and affirmed tentative laws for Lear's world. We saw limitations placed on characters' enlightenment: each father learns only part of what belongs to his own circumstances. We knew all that is common to both old men as well as what is distinctive to each. Whatever understanding of the plight of fathers we finally arrived at, we arrived by an inductive route. Only later did we inquire whether similar terrible laws operated in Jacobean England.

It is perhaps strange that this way of reasoning tended to be more and more associated with naturalist positions. The argument from design is a powerful inductive argument for the existence of God. But when sensitive souls observed actual injustices and brutalities, we were either moved to agonize about God or tempted to distrust the evidence of our own senses and the power of our own reason. Plays and small questions were less terrifying.

The excitement of an inductive discovery in the theater flattered our acuity, invited prediction, and cried to be tested against new experience. Discovery of principles in a dramatic world prepared the way for events that confirmed or repudiated some predictions and (by affording new considerations) refined, amplified, and deepened others. At a play more surely than in life we expected events to validate a satisfying discovery: the mind that organized the data belonged to the same community as ourselves in the audience. Since the playwright had ample opportunity to load the data, his audience expected to find more areas of common agreement and similar response than an equal number of persons would find when confronted with a shared slice of raw actual experience: an audience was more unified than a street full of people. Despite the sense of companionship a congenial audience gives, each of us felt something like the triumph of personal discovery. Each rejoiced in his single inquiring mind, freely adventuring in a world as surprising as his own but orderly enough to make inquiry intellectually and emotionally gratifying.

X INDUCTIVE REASONING AND
A MIDSUMMER NIGHT'S DREAM

LIS. Eigh me: for aught that I could ever reade,
      Could ever here by tale or history,
      The course of true love never did runne smoothe:
      But either it was different in bloud;
HER. Oh crosse! too high to be inthrald to love.
LIS. Or else misgraffed, in respect of yeares;
HER. O spight! too olde to be ingag'd to young.
LIS. Or else, it stoode upon the choyce of friends;
HER. Oh hell, to choose love by anothers eyes!
LYS. Or, if there were a sympathy in choyce,
      Warre, death or sicknesse, did lay siege to it;
      Making it momentany, as a sound;
      Swift, as a shadowe; short, as any dreame;
      Briefe, as the lightning in the collied night.
      That (in a spleene) unfolds both heaven and earth;
      And, ere a man hath power to say, beholde,
      The jawes of darknesse do devoure it up:
      So quick bright things come to confusion.

(I, i)

THREE characters in *A Midsummer Night's Dream* assured playgoers in 1595, as they assure you now, that Athens, Babylon, and all they contain are not worth inquiry, inductive or other. Bottom, remembering wonderful events in the Athenian wood, says, "Man is but an Asse, if hee goe about expound this dreame." Hippolyta finds the mechanicals' interlude "the silliest stuffe, that ever I heard." Robin Goodfellow belittles the whole play: "this weake and idle theame, / No more yielding but a dreame." Those who chose to do so heard in Bottom, Hippolyta, and Robin the voice of authority soberly prescribing a passive response to the comedy. Most relaxing! But though the *Dream* has power to enchant children and sheriffs, many of us, willing to call the Puck a liar, allowed our minds exercise upon themes not altogether weak.

We who liked to ask large questions and seek answers by the inductive route felt a special invitation. As I said earlier, inductive thought seems to me a highly individual process. I confess I had, like Hamlet, a combination of naturalist aspirations and religious conscience. In this last chapter I shall first recapitulate my theologically biased initial responses and then acknowledge a sequence at the end of which laughter had dissolved my worries.

I did not need much discernment to recognize that, in an Athens containing Oberon, Titania, Robin, and the fairies, spirits influence events. The notion that I might be witnessing a cosmic comedy began to dawn on me when I heard Titania bemoan the misplaced seasons and the excessive rain. Noah and Aeneas, I remembered, endured falling weather precipitated by divine anger. I said to myself, "But the play has not shown a drop of water. Hermia has complained of a 'want of raine.' The plans laid by Theseus, Hippolyta, Lysander, Hermia, and Quince's whole crew of actors imply good days and nights out of doors. Why Titania's dismal weather report?" In my answer I recognized that I was imitating the form of Lysander's argument that the course of true love does not run smooth. "By Jove," I said to myself, "people are making the heavy weather that counts. Egeus' tyranny over his daughter, Theseus' harsh legalism, Demetrius' fickleness, Helena's treachery—such behavior, out of kilter and out of character, reflects Oberon's disordered household. Surely we'll see more oddities."

A few minutes later I saw Demetrius come in, Helena hot after him, and heard her disgusted comment:

> Apollo flies and Daphne holds the chase:
> The Dove pursues the Griffon: the milde Hinde
> Makes speede to catch the Tigre. Bootelesse speede,
> When cowardise pursues, and valour flies.

I hardly knew which delighted me more, the comedy or my own brilliant prediction.

"Yet the deities' quarrel," I later mused, "has to be coupled with their other actions in a single community of occasions." I noticed that Oberon and Titania meddle directly with things on the Athenian earth. Titania supervises the welfare of flowers. Oberon takes sides with Helena. Both are bent on making Theseus' and Hippolyta's wedding happy. Joys as well as griefs and insanities in Athens perhaps depend on Oberon's and Titania's passions.

I heard a pun in Robin's "What fooles these mortals bee!" Robin was talking about young lovers, but his words fit the artisans too, and even Theseus. The mortals' crazy behavior shows them fools in the commonest sense. I also took *fools* to mean helpless puppets, as in Romeo's anguished "O I am fortune's fool!" (*Romeo and Juliet*, III, i, 141) Robin, I thought, speaks with bad grace. He himself is a tool of the same natural force that has afflicted the mortals with midsummer madness.

Remembering my wonder how far men are to blame for acts of

God in my English world, I reflected that a *Dream* theology must belittle human responsibility. Athenian mortals' wickedness, like troubles and joys, spins off from fairy discord. So when Oberon and Titania at length agree and Athenians grow virtuous as well as happy, I chuckled, "O my prophetic soul!"

I became aware of questions corresponding to questions in basic theology, the first of which involves nature's reliability, a necessary postulate for all experimental investigators. Not a few Elizabethan Christians believed that good deeds help a fellow thrive on earth and reach heaven. But others, especially Calvinists, argued that God is not subject to persuasion, that human righteousness is but filthy rags, futile attempts to bribe God. Good things come to the just and the unjust, and so do bad things. I observed that mischievous Robin perpetrates mischief on Bottom and his friends simply because he notices an opportunity. Bottom does nothing to deserve translation. The lovers do nothing to earn help. Athens mimics Calvinists' grace and election, I decided, but mimics it gaily and indeed sympathetically, without venom.

Whereas in Calvin's world, under an omniscient, omnipotent God, the interesting question about trouble concerns God's benevolence, in Lysander's world the interesting question concerns Oberon's knowledge and power. Though Oberon knows more than men, and lays plans, he learns about an event only after it has happened. Though more powerful than men, he is not all-powerful. He obeys the cycle of day and night. He controls Titania, Robin, and men by perseverance and resourcefulness rather than by absolute authority. When he takes an interest, however, Oberon can bring a mortal's plan to a better fruition than the mortal intended.

Still proceeding inductively, I asked another question, resembling the logical problem whether anything in a benevolent and omnipotent God's world can be really bad.[1] I knew well the Christian rationalizations: trouble strengthens the character, as when Israel endured the wilderness; it tests men's allegiance to God, as when Abraham consented to sacrifice Isaac; it clarifies values, as when Adam and Eve were expelled from Eden; and so on. No such explanation of trouble appeared to fit Oberon's Athens.

An explanation that does fit, so I reflected, is that pain may prevent or rectify more serious troubles. I remembered a common medical doctrine, phrased in Shakespeare's Sonnet 118: "We sicken to shun sickness when we purge." I remembered "The Taming of a Shrew," in which Ferando matches Kate's harsh behavior with even more disagreeable behavior. I remembered Sidney's comment that a comic dramatist's exaggeration combats undesirable traits in men and society.

In Athens, I inferred, disproportion is the form of serious trouble, and temporary exorbitant exaggeration, through what I called Oberon's Law, provides a remedy. The specific serious trouble in Athens is Titania's failure to keep her impulses in healthy proportion. Excessive in one aspect of her love for the changeling boy, she treats him like a pet. She inflates her splendid assertiveness and makes an adversary of her husband.

Oberon's Law might conceivably operate to cure Titania without Oberon's stir, as a child coming in from the cold learns moderation at the fire place. When Titania is her true self she loves all things and all people, helping them to health, beauty, and (when they have the capacity) love. When she asserts authority excessively, the first result (if it is real) is bad weather. She dislikes the disturbance, and she knows its causes, but bad weather does not cure her. Human evils—Athenian errors in judgment and value, unloving acts by Egeus, Theseus, Demetrius, and the rest—are of a piece with other wretched conditions. Titania still does not behave temperately.

Oberon remonstrates to no avail, then enforces his law. With the help of accident he puts Bottom in Titania's arms, and for a while she embraces that acme of disproportion. Her disorderly impulse surfeits, sickens, and so dies. Healthy impulses return. In the restored harmony of Athens every Athenian, with the momentary exception of Egeus, is again fairly humane, loving, and able to act to his own and his friends' advantage.

While using my primitive inductive routine to phrase curiosity about Athenian world structure, I was aware that the play plays subtly with the confidence which the Athenians repose in naturalist procedures. They do not draw entirely accurate inferences when they appeal to the inductive pattern. Egeus does not prove Hermia's bewitchment. Lysander predicts white water for true love, but the course of his love eventually runs smooth indeed.

I had laughed off antiuniversity diatribes branding new philosophers dangerous atheists. But I privately wondered whether exclusive practice in the new mode might allow one's religious and moral muscles to atrophy. In an inductive inquiry I knew I was content with a limited rather than cosmic context. In political moments, as when I studied Machiavelli, equally as in devout moments, I could wholeheartedly endorse John Donne's objection to treating any man as an island. But reasoning inductively to a valid conclusion differs from understanding an event as a manifestation of God's mind, and it troubled me to reflect that perhaps complete literal obedience to the first and greatest commandment (love God) was a requisite to consistent exercise of the second, the social commandment that makes personal loyalties dependable.

Such a thought colored my laughter when I saw Lysander abandon delectable Hermia. In refuting Egeus Lysander appeals to no god. He binds himself to Hermia (later to Helena) by empty oaths aplenty but none by any god, let alone the right god. I would not concede that naturalist procedures necessarily destroy religious faith, and I was generations too early to dream of astronomer Pierre Simone de Laplace's curt dismissal of God. But the Elizabethan Age was exactly right for the conjecture that those who ignore God may prove socially irresponsible. There was pleasure in entertaining that conjecture—not in fear of a stern Jehovah but in laughter at a Lysander whose irresponsibility does not matter.

More insistently than the moral problem, a question about validity in inquiries into nature concerned me: what does one trust when observations support a proposition belied by revealed truth? I remembered Hermia's words, "I would my father lookt but with my eyes," and Helena's "Love lookes not with the eyes, but with the minde." In the actual world naturalists well know that often two people looking at what both call one and the same thing see two different things. In times past I had noticed two theologians looking at one scriptural text and seeing two different revealed truths, and I should dearly like to report that memory of theological disputes mitigated my worry over naturalist reliance on what is seen with physical eyes. Alack, I did not take that sort of comfort.

The question about trusting the senses, I thought, goes beyond the mere possibility of honest error. Does data perceived by the senses indeed record anything other than behavior of the senses? I remembered the sequence when sleepy Athenians proceed to a stage-sized plot of ground all parts of which are simultaneously represented by an ordinary flat stage floor. Lysander complains that he has fallen "in darke uneaven way," and Demetrius measures his length on "this cold bed." But when Titania brings in Bottom she invites him to "this flowry bed." Titania, the Athenian aristocrats, and Bottom are of course enchanted, but their differing perceptions left me uninformed as to whether the Athenian wooded terrain had any actuality of its own, independent of observers.

I recalled Digges talking about Copernicus and saying, like Epicurus, that the man who sees modifies the thing seen according to the particular way his expectations have been trained. I knew that Copernicus, like the good naturalist leaving Truth for other occasions, had constructed something more modest: a model to account for available mathematical data on celestial motions. But if a model differs from accepted Truth (I kept worrying about this point) does the concept of Truth perhaps call the model and even the observations themselves into serious question?

I remembered from *Romeo and Juliet* Juliet's disquisition on names and roses. Something in the comedy—possibly Titania's response to Bottom's long-nosed voice, "What Angell wakes me

. . . sing againe," recalling Romeo's "Speak again, bright angel!" (*Romeo and Juliet*, II, ii, 26), or possibly the friar's comment (so intriguingly different from Helena's), "Young men's love then lies / Not truly in their hearts, but in their eyes," (*Romeo and Juliet*, II, iii, 67–68)—something, anyhow, reminded me of that tragedy of lovers who will not see each other through their fathers' eyes, of a Tybalt who will not see Romeo as Romeo but as a Montague, and finally of a Romeo who, bent on death, cannot tell a live girl from a corpse.

By the time I had followed the play back from the wood to Athens I was prepared to hear Theseus, in his lovely naturalist introduction to the final scene, rejecting the truth of his organic world, lumping Oberon and Titania together with other pitiful illusions:

> I never may beleeve
> These antique fables, nor these Fairy toyes.
> Lovers, and mad men have such seething braines,
> Such shaping phantasies, that apprehend more,
> Then coole reason ever comprehends. The lunatick,
> The lover, and the Poet are of imagination all compact.
> One sees more divels, then vast hell can holde:
> That is the mad man. The lover, all as frantick,
> Sees Helens beauty in a brow of Aegypt.
> The Poets eye, in a fine frenzy, rolling, doth glance
> From heaven to earth, from earth to heaven. And as
> Imagination bodies forth the formes of things
> Unknowne: the Poets penne turnes them to shapes,
> And gives to ayery nothing, a locall habitation,
> And a name. Such trickes hath strong imagination,
> That if it would but apprehend some joy,
> It comprehends some bringer of that joy.
> Or in the night, imagining some feare,
> How easie is a bush suppos'd a Beare?

As Theseus by edict futilely banishes spiritual causes from the Athenian story, he utters a right prologue for "Pyramus and Thisby."

To my mind, still not completely wedded to the new philosophy that I found exciting, and familiar with Sir Philip Sidney's *Defence of Poesy*, Theseus sounded like Epicurus and like Dee

at Mortlake and Marlowe at Ralegh's, decrying any reality except measured facts organized by cool reason into fresh generali-
zations. Sidney, though he acknowledges faults in wholly fanciful constructions, says that the poet's imagination organizes
into warm fictions cold facts for which he has ransacked earth
and the heavens. Sidney calls the astronomer who claims to
measure the distances of the stars a greater liar than the poet
who, however persuasive, makes no claim to state new facts.[2] It
seemed to me that the naturalist philosopher's model, the as-
trologer's constellations, and the poet's fiction equally exemplify (as does, perhaps, the lover's love but not the lunatic's hal-
lucination) the shaping function of mind imposing order upon
data, which the term *imagination* designates as well as any
other. I went a little farther than Sidney as I supposed the
natural philosopher more vulnerable to the creative impulse
than the poet, who makes his fiction and leaves it. The investigator trusts his model as it serves him, and having thereby
come to love it, feels tender toward it, like a mother.

I could not censure Theseus. Outside the theater I had applauded naturalist friends for dismissing untestable assertions.
Undue friendliness to propositions deriving plausibly and inductively but unacceptably from undisputed facts was already
an embarrassing temptation in the sixteenth century, and the
kind thing to do with people who claimed scientific demonstration of foolish positions was to ignore them. Theseus thus ignores Hippolyta's suggestion:

> All the story of the night told over,
> And all their minds transfigur'd so together
> More witnesseth than fancies images,
> And growes to something of great constancy:
> But howsoever, strange and admirable.

In Athens sane Theseus (sustaining due skepticism, putting the
burden of proof where it belongs) is as wrong as he would be
right in Babylon. Contrariwise Hippolyta, a woman, a born bar-
barian, obviously the wrong person for superior logic, exemplifies the precious second article of the naturalist creed, respect

for unexpected data. Using an inductive argument, she begins to have a valid understanding of her world.

I knew that outside comedy Hippolyta's words would be evidence of gullibility, Theseus' words eloquently right. But for the moment, like the ancient Skeptics, I was ready to concede that I could not know what indeed is the ultimate structure of the world that contains my beloved England. In a mood less confident than faith or hope, I had a decided preference.

I mused on the structure of "Pyramus," exhibiting human passion and frustration at the beginning and middle, and at the end death without babies. Prompted perhaps by the name *Limander* recalling Anaximander, I saw its world, given brief form by hot passion, subsiding into chaos. I preferred to think that England is in a history whose structure, like the Athenian play, leads through cycles toward joy.

EPILOGUE

DESPITE his persistent sympathy with naturalist Lysander, our judicious young man of law came to the end of *A Midsummer Night's Dream* laughing a magnanimous laughter. He had just a moment earlier joined Lysander in a contemptuous laughter at a Pyramus and Thisby whom superstitions blind to the facts of their world. He remembered he had laughed when Lysander in the wood, ignorant of Oberon and Robin Goodfellow, trusts his enchanted eyes and his reason. He noticed that Lysander, continuing to exemplify the complete naturalist's habit of sifting out all data not congenial with his peculiar chosen receptors, remains till the end as ignorant of his own world as braying Bottom—maybe a shade more ignorant. Nor does Lysander even recognize in Thisby's Babylon a *reductio ad absurdum* of his own views. Since our young playgoer allowed himself to laugh at what is funny, he laughed now at laughing Lysander, laughed at the laughter of a disbeliever, laughed at the laughter that was still coming from his own disbelieving mouth—a superior, satirical, if friendly, condescending laughter. He was laughing, as Sidney and Frye could wish, at an exaggerated portrait of himself at his most brave and philosophic moment. That was not all.

The play had taught his mind no solution to cosmic mystery. Yet it had taught him. No closer now to replacing ignorance with knowledge, not prompted to reform his life, not squirming at being found out, he came to play's end having in himself achieved a completion more satisfying even than the sweet fool's paradise completed for the confident Athenians. He was laughing lightly now at a predicament that had caused him grim exasperation. The very names of the Athenians who offered a lively reference point for his laughter, originally startling in their fractured evocation of lovers and battles long ago and modern citizens, now sounded simply right. Oberon's hierarchy, originally perceived as a diminutive cento from known myths, now felt right for this Athens. The sense of rightness was a species of love. It was an expansive love, extending beyond the ignorant fictional Athenians to encompass his live, earnest, philosophic friends, himself, and even the world predicament they shared. He saw frustrations with a new patience. He understood them with a newly compassionate heart. While the play still embraced him in the roster of those it enchants, he supposed he could laugh with rich delight.

Throughout the evening the delight clung to him and would not go away. When, at evening's end, he leaned from bed and blew out the candle, properly and happily married as he was, he smiled at his fancy that the joy, fruitfulness, and peace of his bed were assured to him by Titania and Oberon. For a fleeting moment he felt he knew nothing, like Socrates. As he fell asleep his laughter, God willing, was not arrogant but gratified, not harsh but silent, serene, and perhaps cosmic.

NOTES

Prologue

1. Henry Adams, *Mont-Saint-Michel and Chartres* (Boston: Houghton Mifflin, 1933), 144.

2. The year 1595 fits the conditions important in this book. So does a date a year or two earlier, and so does any date in 1596 and 1597, prior to Meres's *Palladis Tamia* of 1598, which mentions the play.

3. R. C. Collingwood, in *The Idea of History* (Oxford: Clarendon Press, 1946), speaks of history as the reliving of a past event so as to know oneself well. I am in debt to Collingwood.

4. See Alfred Harbage, *Shakespeare's Audience* (New York: Columbia University Press, 1941), and his *Shakespeare and the Rival Traditions* (New York: Macmillan, 1952).

5. Low-keyed books that describe country and village life include: Henry N. Ellacombe, *The Plant Lore and Garden Craft of Shakespeare* (London: E. Arnold, 1896); Sidney Lee, *Stratford on Avon* (London: Seeley, 1890); and Allardyce Nicoll, *The Elizabethans* (Cambridge: Cambridge University Press, 1957).

6. Many observe decorum. Nevill Coghill in *Shakespeare's Professional Skills* (Cambridge: Cambridge University Press, 1964), for example, acknowledges that "Shakespeare achieved a synthesis by means unimaginable to us who are not Shakespeare" (p. 41), yet he says that "very early in his career, a 'comedy' came to mean, for Shakespeare, a love-story: fresh from his first creations in comic form . . . he knew it was safe to plot a play on the mutual loves of Jack and Jill" (p. 57). Critics in this tradition sometimes phrase an arguable interpretation as fact, as when Coghill says, "Theseus, in Chaucer as in Shakespeare, is a piece of warm greatness and stability, the unmoved mover of the human side of both stories" (p. 53).

In this book we shall not read the mind of any author, including Shakespeare. If we say, for example, "By making his Babylon more agreeable than Ovid's, Chaucer emphasizes Tisbe's sacrifice," we shall be reading the mind of an imagined Elizabethan who has read Ovid and Chaucer. If we say, "Shakespeare's Babylon is more desolate than Ovid's," we shall not be proclaiming final truth. We shall be looking at the artisans' "Pyramus and Thisby" through eyes familiar with books popular in 1595.

7. Alfred North Whitehead, *Science and the Modern World* (New York: Macmillan, 1950), 65.

Introduction

1. John M. Ziman, *Public Knowledge: An Essay Concerning the Social Dimension of Science* (London: Cambridge University Press, 1968). For a classic instance, see pages 50–51 and note on page 36: "A good experiment is a powerful piece of rhetoric; it has the ability to persuade the most obdurate and skeptical mind to accept a new idea; it makes a positive contribution to public knowledge."

2. Werner Heisenberg, *Physics and Philosophy: The Revolution in Modern*

Science, ed. Ruth Nanda Anshen (New York: Harper, 1958); Michael Polanyi, *Personal Knowledge* (Chicago: University of Chicago Press, 1958).

3. C. L. Barber, *Shakespeare's Festive Comedy* (Princeton: Princeton University Press, 1959); David P. Young, *Something of Great Constancy* (New Haven: Yale University Press, 1966), and Jackson I. Cope, *The Theater and the Dream* (Baltimore: Johns Hopkins University Press, 1973), esp. 219–25.

4. Rosemond Tuve, *Elizabethan and Metaphysical Imagery* (Chicago: University of Chicago Press, 1947), 104.

Chapter I

1. All quotations from *A Midsummer Night's Dream* are transcribed from a photostat copy of the Thomas Fisher Quarto, London, 1600, in the Folger Shakespeare Library, Washington, D.C. I modernize *j, s, u,* and *v* and do not reproduce italics. All other Shakespeare texts are from William Allen Neilson and Charles Jarvis Hill (eds.), *The Complete Plays and Poems of William Shakespeare* (Boston: Houghton Mifflin, 1942). In quoting from other English authors I modernize spelling except where I would falsify something I am examining.

2. Critics have looked elsewhere for unity, and some have found it. From a posture different from our playgoer's, for example, James L. Calderwood, in *Shakespearean Metadrama* (Minneapolis: University of Minnesota Press, 1971), persuasively describes a fully organized "theatrical interaction of playwright, play, and audience" (p. 19).

Others have praised the "prettily interwoven" plots or their "skillful interweaving." See William Shakespeare, *A Midsummer Night's Dream,* ed. Sir Arthur Quiller-Couch and John Dover Wilson (Cambridge: Cambridge University Press, 1924), xviii, hereinafter cited as Cambridge edition; and Hardin Craig and David Bevington (eds.), *The Complete Works of Shakespeare* (Rev. ed.; Glenview, Ill.: Scott Foresman, 1973), 182.

In Dover Wilson's view Shakespeare revised his play for a wedding festivity by tacking on, after Theseus disperses the couples to their beds, an epithalamion superfluous to giving every Jack civil permission to have his right Jill. It is not superfluous to the picture of a changed Athenian world. See Cambridge edition, ix–xi and 151.

Some years ago Robert Adger Law observed that the plots are not adequately interwoven: "What I wish to stress is that Shakespeare here is . . . handling four separate groups of figures . . . [that] remain solidified and independent of each other at the last as at the first." See Robert Adger Law, "The 'Pre-Conceived Pattern' of *A Midsummer Night's Dream,*" in *Studies in English* (Austin: University of Texas Press, 1943), 7. Law is retorting to a case for unity made by Thomas Marc Parrott, *Shakespeare: Twenty-Three Plays and the Sonnets* (Rev. ed.; New York: Scribner, 1953), 132.

William Empson has demonstrated a unity arising from analogies between the actions of two groups of characters in a single play. Richard Levin, amplifying Empson's principles, sets forth a philosophical rationale for a unity he observes in *A Midsummer Night's Dream.* We owe much to Empson and Levin, yet in critical inquiries of a kind that Levin finds old-fashioned there remains no little merit. For example, Madeleine Doran aptly points out that "each of the plots . . . touches one of the others at some point." If we merely add from sixteenth-century commonplaces the passion to discern correspondences (noted for example by Thomas B. Stroup) and the reinforcing assumption that earthly events happen because of celestial or infernal events, we are on the brink of perceiving that Oberon and Titania are in the classical sense the unifying cause of all that happens in Athens. See Thomas B. Stroup, *Microcosmos: The Shape of the Elizabethan Play* (Lexington: University of Kentucky Press, 1965); William Empson, "Double Plots: Heroic and Pastoral in Main Plot and Sub Plot," in his *Some Versions of Pastoral* (London: Chatto and Windus, 1935); Richard Levin, *The Multiple Plot in English Renaissance Drama* (Chicago: University of Chicago Press, 1971), esp. 10–20; and Madeleine Doran's comment in Alfred Harbage (ed.), *William Shakespeare: The Complete Works* (Baltimore: Penguin, 1969), 146.

3. This way of thinking about history has been commonly ascribed to Greeks since St. Augustine. See Karl Löwith, *Meaning in History* (Chicago: University of Chicago Press, 1949). Instances supporting the generalization are in Polybius, *The Histories* (Loeb Classical Library ed.; London: William Heinemann, 1922–27), Bk. VI, Sects. 9, 51, 57, and Bk. III, Sects. 289, 385, 397.

Though Anaximander may envision an utterly mindless world, the pattern of cyclical return was in the sixteenth century often taken as evidence of cosmic mind. See Michael Macklem, *The Anatomy of the World* (Minneapolis: University of Minnesota Press, 1958). The notion is discussed in a wide context in Mircea Eliade, *The Myth of the Eternal Return: Or Cosmos and History*, trans. Willard R. Trask (New York: Pantheon, 1954).

4. The city was often called "the town" as in Hubert Hall, *Society in the Elizabethan Age* (3rd ed.; New York: Macmillan, n.d. [ca. 1890]).

5. The doctrine was familiar in the words of Sir Thomas Elyot. In *The Boke, Named the Governour* (1531; facsim. rpt.; Menston, Eng.: Scolar Press, 1970), Bk. I, Chap. 1, Fol. 4–5, he says that those "excelling in knowledge whereby other[s] be governed be ministers for the only profit and commodity of them which have not equal understanding: where they which do exercise artificial science or corporal labour do not travail for their superiors only but also for their own necessity. So the husbandman feedeth himself and the cloth maker: the cloth maker appareleth himself and the husband: they both succor other artificers: other artificers them: they and other artificers them that be governors."

6. This commonplace resides behind the whole of Richard Hooker's *Of the Laws of Ecclesiastical Polity*, whose first four books appeared in 1594. See, for instance (Everyman rpt.; London: J. M. Dent, 1925), Bk. I, Chap. 2.

7. A common metaphor called the world a book expressing God as surely as Scripture. Shakespeare's audience was thus prepared to understand the Athenian world as a book expressing Oberon's nature, expressing the household economy of fairyland. Theseus and the rest were, in effect, funny because they could not read their own book of nature. Sir Walter Ralegh's eloquent statement, written twenty years after *A Midsummer Night's Dream*, establishes at once the antiquity and the persistence of the concept. In *The Historie of the World* (1614; rpt. London: G. Lathum and R. Young, 1628), Pt. I, Bk. I, Chap. 1, Sect. 1, he says: "But by his own word, and by this visible world, is God perceived of men; which is also the understood language of the Almighty, vouchsafed to all his creatures, whose hieroglyphical characters, are the unnumbered stars, the sun and moon, written on these large volumes of the firmament: written also on the earth and the seas, by the letters of all those living creatures, and plants, which inhabit and reside therein. Therefore said that learned Cusanus, *Mundus universus nihil aliud est, quam Deus explicatus*; the world universal is nothing else but God expressed." However,

the concept was old when "Cusanus" was born. Michel de Montaigne quotes Manilius and Saint Paul to support his defense of Raymond Sebond's study of the nature of God through observing "in the things of this world, some image resembling, after a sort, the workman who built and shaped them." The world Montaigne describes is not a book but a temple with statues whose architect is God. *The Essays of Montaigne*, trans. George B. Ives (4 vols.; Cambridge, Mass.: Harvard University Press, 1925), II, 194. Montaigne proceeds to question whether men's interpretation of God's architecture can be depended on. So did Shakespeare's judicious playgoers.

8. Romans, 13:10.

9. Quoted from C. F. Tucker Brooke and Nathaniel Burton Paradise (eds.), *English Drama, 1580–1642* (New York: D. C. Heath, 1933).

10. Thorndike describes devices to "bridge the chasm between the actuality of the pit and the illusion of the stage." Ashley H. Thorndike, *English Comedy* (New York: Cooper Square Publishers, 1965), 102. See T. Walter Herbert, "Dislocation and the Modest Demand in *A Midsummer Night's Dream*," in George Walton Williams (ed.), *Renaissance Papers, 1961* (Durham, N.C.: Southeastern Renaissance Conference, 1962).

11. Two who have described the play as part of a wedding celebration are Paul N. Siegel, "*A Midsummer Night's Dream* and the Wedding Guests," *Shakespeare Quarterly*, IV (1953), 139–44; and Paul A. Olson, "*A Midsummer Night's Dream* and the Meaning of Court Marriage," *Journal of English Literary History* XXIV (1957), 95–119.

12. F. N. Robinson (ed.), *The Complete Works of Geoffrey Chaucer* (Boston: Houghton Mifflin, 1933).

13. In *The Taming of the Shrew* Shakespeare employs Peele's trick with a difference. The anonymous *Taming of a Shrew* parallels Peele by having a prankster lord, after presenting the shrew-taming show before the common drunk, redeliver him to his spot by the tavern. Shakespeare gives his Sly no lines after that eager inebriate has served to invite the large audience to regard the Petruchio-Kate delinquencies with the detached tolerance given a narrated practical joke. At the end of Shakespeare's *Taming of the Shrew* the audience may, if the director chooses, forget that Kate's submission is supposed to be credible only to an alcoholized imagination. A skillful actress makes the last scene wonderfully ambiguous, inducing the judicious playgoer to laugh at his own thoughts about the married condition.

Chapter II

1. Sir Philip Sidney, arguing in *The Defence of Poesie* (London, 1595) that poets do not lie when they invent fictions, speaks of names:

But hereto is replied, that the poets give names to men they write of, which argueth a conceit of an actual truth, and so, not being true, proveth a falsehood. And doth the lawyer lie then, when under the names of "John of the Stile" and "John of the Nokes" he putteth his case? But that is easily answered. Their naming of men is but to make their picture more lively, and not to build any history. . . . We see we cannot play at chess but that we must give names to our chessmen; and yet, methinks, he were a very partial champion of truth that would say we lied for giving a piece of wood the reverend title of a bishop. The poet nameth Cyrus and Aeneas, no other way than to show what men of their fames, fortunes, and estates should do.

See Sir Philip Sidney, *The Defence of Poesie*, ed. Albert Feuillerat (Cambridge: Cambridge University Press, 1923), 29–30.

In devising names for *A Midsummer Night's Dream* Shakespeare exemplifies Elizabethan "invention"—imitating an earlier structure but with such freedom that the new has an identity of its own, resembling the model as a child resembles its parent, not precisely but recognizably.

2. That Shakespeare played with his own name elsewhere than in sonnets like 135 and 136, I have speculated in "The Naming of Falstaff," *Emory University Quarterly*, X (March, 1954), 1–10.

3. For a good recent and different approach to dream as a device see Marjorie B. Garber, *Dream in Shakespeare* (New Haven: Yale University Press, 1974).

4. F. N. Robinson (ed.), *The Complete Works of Geoffrey Chaucer* (Boston: Houghton Mifflin, 1933). 781.

5. *Ibid.*, 780.

Chapter III

1. See T. Walter Herbert, "Shakespeare Announces a Ghost," *Shakespeare Quarterly*, I (October, 1950), 247–54.

2. Joseph Addison, *The Spectator* (London: H. Washbourne, 1857), 482–83. Addison is charming, but how different from an Elizabethan he sounds when he says in the same *Spectator* paper: "We are pleased with surveying the different habits and behaviours of foreign countries: how much more must we be delighted and surprised when we are led, as it were, into a new creation, and see the persons and manners of another species!"

3. Sixteenth-century *India*, like Chaucer's *Inde* associated with the Indus River, often (as the Oxford English Dictionary suggests) signified the territory beyond the Indus, but at times it meant something even less definite: lands to the east of the vague boundary of the Holy Land and east of "the East" that Antony speaks of as the home of Cleopatra. See the introduction by S. L. Lee in *The Boke of Duke Huon of Bordeaux*, trans. Sir John Bourchier, Lord Berners (*ca.* 1534; London: N. Trubner, 1882–87), li.

4. C. S. Lewis, *A Preface to Paradise Lost* (New York: Oxford University Press, 1961), 57.

5. Isaac Reed (ed.), *The Plays of William Shakespeare*, with notes by Samuel Johnson and George Steevens, (10 vols.; London: C. Bathurst, 1785), I, 16.

6. Reginald Scot, *The Discoverie of Witchcraft* (1584; London: J. Rodker, 1930), Bk. VII, Chap. 15, p. 86.

7. Thomas Keightley, *The Fairy Mythology* (Rev. ed., 1850; London: G. Bell, 1910), 290.

8. Ronald B. McKerrow (ed.), *The Works of Thomas Nashe* (5 vols.; London: Sidgwick and Jackson, 1910), I, 347.

9. Scot, *Discoverie*, Bk. III, Chap. 2, p. 24.

10. See James Orchard Halliwell, *Illustrations of the Fairy Mythology of "A Midsummer Night's Dream"* (London: The Shakespeare Society, 1845).

11. Accounts of Robin are in Minor White Latham, *The Elizabethan Fairies* (New York: Columbia University Press, 1930), esp. 218–62; and Katharine M. Briggs, *The Anatomy of Puck* (London: Routledge and Paul, 1959), esp. 75–81.

12. See Latham, *Fairies*, 65–80; and see Briggs's evidence that tiny fairies may have been known in Britain, *Anatomy*, especially pp. 14–15. Add to this the story about the old ivory chessmen, about two inches tall, now in the

British Museum. When time revealed an ancient closed room, a man entered, saw the chessmen and fled, assuming they were fairies.

13. Howard Horace Furness (ed.), in *A New Variorum Edition of Shakespeare* (24 vols.; Philadelphia: Lippincott, 1895), X, 127–28, summarizes what White says and agrees with him.

14. William Shakespeare, *A Midsummer Night's Dream*, ed. Henry Cuningham (London: Methuen, 1905), 78. *Moth* is glossed *mote* in William Shakespeare, *A Midsummer Night's Dream*, ed. Sir Arthur Quiller-Couch and John Dover Wilson (Cambridge: Cambridge University Press, 1924), 173; and in George Lyman Kittredge and Irving Ribner (eds.), *The Complete Works of Shakespeare* (Waltham, Mass.: Ginn, 1971), 233. That the meaning is probably *speck* or *mote* say Wolfgang Clemen in Sylvan Barnet (ed.), *The Complete Signet Classic Shakespeare* (New York: Harcourt Brace Jovanovich, 1972), 541; Madeleine Doran in Alfred Harbage (ed.), *William Shakespeare: The Complete Works* (Baltimore: Penguin, 1969), 160; and Blakemore Evans (ed.), *The Riverside Shakespeare* (Boston: Houghton Mifflin, 1974), 233. In Hardin Craig and David Bevington (eds.), *The Complete Works of Shakespeare* (Rev. ed.; Glenview, Ill.: Scott Foresman, 1973) *Moth* is printed without comment.

15. Chaucer's Wife of Bath resented churchmen's hostility to the fairies, and Reginald Scot attests the fears fairies stirred in children. Although King James thought fairies counseled with witches, he had never arrested a fairy. A poor woman could become a witch but not a fairy. See King James the First, *Daemonologie*, ed. G. B. Harrison (New York: Barnes and Noble, 1966), 73 ff.

16. Halliwell's *Illustrations* provides a good introduction to the behavior of fairy ladies.

17. A carnal Bottom is not unthinkable in the latter years of the twentieth century. In Peter Brook's uproarious production Bottom was as lusty as you please. The quality of Brook's laughter is perhaps closer to the Elizabethans than the clownish coyness and evanescent gossamer occasionally sought for the play by producers and directors a generation or two ago. But in regaining contact with sixteenth-century flesh and bone we need not feel compelled to abjure their other fun. Enough memories of missed opportunities still linger in enough men to make Bottom's obtuseness to Titania's offers worth presenting for the friendly laughter his hearty ways invite.

In Jan Kott's essay "Titania and the Ass's Head," in *Shakespeare Our Contemporary* (Garden City, N.Y.: Doubleday, 1964) Bottom is not even happy in his sexuality. Kott calls *A Midsummer Night's Dream* "the most erotic of Shakespeare's plays" and finds the eroticism "expressed . . . brutally." In his eyes "the behaviour of all the characters . . . is promiscuous" (p. 214). His Hermia goes to sleep drunk with Lysander and wakes ashamed. His Bottom is monstrously bestial. "If one can see humour in the scenes between Titania and Bottom," says Kott, "it is the English kind of humour, 'humeur noir,' cruel and scatalogical." Kott describes a joyless play. Hugh N. Richmond, in *Shakespeare's Sexual Comedy* (Indianapolis: Bobbs-Merrill, 1971) describes a more cheerful Bottom in a more cheerful play.

18. King James, *Daemonologie*, 73; cited by Keightley, *Fairy Mythology*, 325. King James and Keightley, who wrote in 1833, have generally prevailed with subsequent editors. See for instance T. F. Thiselton-Dyer, *Folk Lore of Shakespeare* (London: Griffith and Farron, 1883), 4; Frank Sidgwick, *Sources and Analogues of "A Midsummer Night's Dream"* (New York: Duffield, 1908), 36; and Dover Wilson and Quiller-Couch, Cambridge edition, 103. T. S. Baynes, in *Shakespeare Studies* (London: Longmans Green, 1894), 210 ff., points out that "in reality the name (Titania) occurs not once only, but several

times, not as the designation of a single goddess, but of several female deities, supreme or subordinate, descended from the Titans." Baynes's much-neglected comment is worth reading at length.

19. The dominion of the earliest fairy, Elfin, included "all India" and America. Francis J. Child (ed.), *The Poetical Works of Edmund Spenser* (Boston: Little Brown, 1864), Bk. II, Canto x, Stanzas 71–72; Bk. II, 103.

20. Ovid, *Metamorphoses* (Loeb Classical Library ed.; 2 vols.; London: William Heinemann, 1921), Vol. I, Bk. III, line 173. Subsequent citations in the text refer to Volume I and are indicated by book and line numbers in parentheses.

21. Plutarch tells the story in his *Life of Theseus*.

22. Virgil's *Aeneid*, in *Virgil* (Loeb Classical Library ed.; 2 vols.; London: William Heinemann, 1965), I, 242 ff.

Prefiguring the dripping consequences of Titania's temporary success in headstrong behavior and the result of reconciliation with Oberon, Stephan Batman, in *The Golden Booke of the Leaden Goddes* (London: Thomas Marshe, 1577), A2, records a sixteenth-century notion about Juno and Jupiter: "Jupiter and Juno are said to be at variance, because Jupiter being hot and dry, not having his heat repressed with moistness, all things are burned and parched; again, when Juno's moistness is not qualified with Jupiter's heat, all things are drowned and overflowed; but when their qualities are with equal temperance combined together, then the earth doth yield her fruits with great plenty and abundance."

23. C. F. Tucker Brooke (ed.), *The Works of Christopher Marlowe* (Oxford: Clarendon Press, 1910), 401.

24. Divine benevolence expressing itself in natural order was a frequent corollary of the organic concept of the world. It has roots in innumerable revered statements in Pythagorean notions about music and in Saint Paul's Epistles to the Romans and Corinthians. It found expression in many lyric passages: in Spenser's "Hymn in Honour of Love," and in Lorenzo and Jessica's Belmont antiphony.

25. See the note in Hyder E. Rollins (ed.), *Tottel's Miscellany, or Songes and Sonnettes written by the ryght honorable Lorde Henry Hawarde late Earle of Surrey, and other* (2 vols.; Cambridge: Harvard University Press, 1929), II, 265–66.

26. See, for example, *Malleus Maleficarum*, trans. Montague Summers (London: Pushkin, 1951) 147–49. See also Scot's *Discoverie of Witchcraft*, 19.

27. As might be expected from anything connected with this teasing play, *seven* is ambiguous, being at times the number of sin. See V. F. Hopper, *Medieval Number Symbolism* (New York: Columbia University Press, 1938), 84–85.

28. A now amusing section in the prevailingly frightful *Malleus Maleficarum*, 41–48, develops this proposition.

29. *Malleus Maleficarum*, 96–102 and *passim*.

30. An exception is recounted by Scot, *Discoverie of Witchcraft*, 54, in a story about a sailor's encounter with a witch who made an ass of him.

Chapter IV

1. Neither Ovid nor Shakespeare had any inkling that Babylonians at the dawn of history developed a responsible mathematics for business and astronomy. It is tempting, but not necessary, to guess that a heartsick Babylonian had a nightmare about man in a world completely definable by an unpoetic

arithmetician's mind and that he phrased his vision in an original "Pyramus and Thisbe," which made its way, eventually, to Ovid. Decipherment of cuneiform tests began about the middle of the nineteenth century. For a popular account of early mathematics see H. J. J. Winter, *Eastern Science* (London: J. Murray, 1952).

2. Ovid, *Metamorphoses* (Loeb Classical Library ed.; 2 vols.; London: William Heinemann, 1921), Vol. I, Bk. IV, lines 81–82.

3. The Knight's Tale in F. N. Robinson (ed.), *The Complete Works of Geoffrey Chaucer* (Boston: Houghton Mifflin, 1933) lines 773–75.

4. In Richard Hooker, *Of the Laws of Ecclesiastical Polity* (London: J. M. Dent, 1925), Bk. I, Chap. 3. Hooker calls upon the Bible, of course, and among others Aristotle, Hippocrates, and Theophrastus.

5. Of all the documents that evoke sixteenth-century prototypes of this good-naturedly ironic scene (humble folk performing for the highborn, who exhibit lofty condescension), the best I know is *Robert Laneham's Letter, Describing a Part of the Entertainment unto Queen Elizabeth at the Castle of Kenilworth in 1575*. A useful edition was prepared by F. J. Furnivall (London: Chatto and Windus, 1907). It is tempting to imagine that Shakespeare had a copy of the original, not least because Laneham, a mercer, writes like an ebullient Bottom.

6. In the sixteenth century not everyone was fair to the ancients like Democritus and Epicurus, notorious proponents of the godless world. However, consult Lucretius, *De Rerum Natura*, especially Books I and III.

7. There is an argument for restoring the often-emended Quarto reading of Hippolyta's words about the moon. The relevant lines:

> Fower daies will quickly steepe themselves in night:
> Fower nights will quickly dreame away the time:
> And then the Moone, like to a silver bowe,
> Now bent in heaven, shall beholde the night
> Of our solemnities.

Nicholas Rowe and nearly all subsequent editors have changed (or as Malone said, "corrected") "Now bent" to "New bent." They polish the fresh meaning by eliminating the comma after "bowe." Edmond Malone (ed.), *The Plays and Poems of William Shakespeare* (10 vols.; London: J. Rivington, 1790), II, 442.

But the original makes good and equally appropriate sense. "Now" fits other moon allusions in the play. As the Amazon would know, a bent bow is a belligerent bow, a bow in condition for shooting, and Titania at least will speak of the moon as "pale in her anger." If the Quarto had said "New," as the Neilson and Hill note claims, we should of course follow it. William Allen Neilson and Charles Jarvis Hill (eds.), *The Complete Plays and Poems of William Shakespeare* (Boston: Houghton Mifflin, 1942), 90.

8. The case for "behowls" is fully argued by Malone (ed.), *Plays and Poems of Shakespeare*, II, 536.

Chapter V

1. Marjorie Nicolson, *The Breaking of the Circle* (Rev. ed.; New York: Columbia University Press, 1960), 169. If my whole argument appears incompatible with Miss Nicolson's remarks about Shakespeare, it is because we look for different things. She looks for evidence of what authors thought even when they never explicitly said it. I look for the books and interests that formed the minds of playgoers and ask how a representative might respond.

I do not demonstrate anything about Shakespeare's mentality when he constructed the mechanicals' version of "Pyramus and Thisby." Professor Nicolson speculates that Shakespeare abandoned London before he was fifty because he could not stand to think about "a world and a universe that were growing unintelligible." (p. 170) I suppose that as early as 1595 some who attended *A Midsummer Night's Dream* saw that the world might indeed be unintelligible, and shivered. But I think they could stand to think about formidable possibilities.

Those whom the comedy now leaves feeling cheered rather than glum, like the philosopher Professor Nicolson quotes out of Fontanelle (p. 168), may conjecture that some of Donne's friends, glancing at two versions of an unknowable world, might have felt at least less tense after the play than before.

2. In John Donne's "An Anatomie of the World: The First Anniversary," particularly lines 205 ff.

3. Thomas Digges, "A Perfit Description of the Caelestial Orbes according to the most aunciente doctrine of the Pythagoreans, latelye revived by Copernicus and by Geometrical Demonstration approved," being "The Addition" to *A Prognostication everlasting.* . . . Published by Leonard Digges, Gentleman. Lately corrected and augmented by Thomas Digges his sonne (London: Thomas Marshe, 1576), n.3. Ann Arbor, Mich., University Microfilms reprint.

4. I quote from *Nikolaus Kopernikus Gesamtausgabe*, Vol. II of F. Kubach and Karl Zeller (eds.), *De Revolutionibus Orbium Caelestium* (2 vols.; Munich: R. Oldenbourg, 1949), 26.

5. George T. Buckley, *Rationalism in Sixteenth Century English Literature* (Chicago: private ed., 1933), 79.

6. The sketch is in "The Addition" to Digges's *A Prognostication everlasting.*

7. Henry Hallam, *Introduction to the Literature of Europe in the Fifteenth, Sixteenth, and Seventeenth Centuries* (2 vols.; New York: A. C. Armstrong, 1891), II, 323. Hallam describes the delight with which the complete animist Campanella followed Gilbert (III, 19).

8. Thomas Henry Huxley, "William Harvey," *Fortnightly Review*, n.s., XXIII (1878), 185.

9. William Gilbert, *De Magnete*, trans. P. F. Mottelay (1892; rpt. New York: Dover, 1958), Bk. V, Chap. 7, pp. 308–12.

10. *Ibid.* 309–10.

11. C. G. Jung and W. Pauli, *The Interpretation of Nature and the Psyche* (New York: Pantheon, 1955), 156.

12. Arthur Koestler, *The Watershed* (Garden City, N.Y.: Doubleday, 1960), 60. See also Jung and Pauli, *The Interpretation of Nature*, 167 ff.

13. Quoted in Jung and Pauli, *The Interpretation of Nature*, 173. The same Kepler also said, "My aim is to show that the heavenly machine is not a kind of divine, live being, but a kind of clockwork (and he who believes that a clock has a soul, attributes the maker's glory to the work), insofar as nearly all the manifold motions are caused by a most simple, magnetic, and material force, just as all motions of the clock are caused by a simple weight. And I also show how these physical causes are to be given numerical and geometrical expression." Koestler, *The Watershed*, 155.

14. C. Plinius Secundus, *The Historie of the World*, trans. Philemon Holland (1601; rpt. London: I. Grismond, 1635), Bk. II, Chap. 6.

15. *The Works of William Harvey, M.D.*, trans. Robert Wallis, M.D. (London, 1847; New York: Johnson, 1965), 82.

16. *Ibid.*, 83.

17. Richard Hooker, *Of the Laws of Ecclesiastical Polity* (London: J. M. Dent, 1925), Bk. I, Chap. 3, p. 161.

18. Hardin Craig, *The Enchanted Glass: The Elizabethan Mind in Litera-ture* (New York: Oxford University Press, 1936); Theodore Spencer, *Shakes-peare and the Nature of Man* (New York: Macmillan, 1942); E. M. W. Tillyard, *The Elizabethan World Picture* (London: Chatto and Windus, 1943); S. K. Heninger, Jr., *Touches of Sweet Harmony: Pythagorean Cosmology and Re-naissance Poetics* (San Marino, Calif.: Huntington Library, 1974).

19. Hooker, *Polity*, Chap. 2, p. 150.

20. *Ibid.*, Chap. 3, p. 160.

21. *Ibid.*, p. 157.

22. "*Aut Deus naturae patitur, aut mundi machina dissolvetur.*" Quoted by Hooker, *Polity*, Bk. I, Chap. 3, p. 160.

23. William Lawne, *An Abridgement of the Institution of Christian Reli-gion, Written by M. John Calvin*, trans. Christopher Featherstone (Edinburgh: n.p., 1587), 35; Ann Arbor, Mich., University Microfilms reprint.

24. Robert Greene, "A Pleasant Discovery of the Coosenage of Colliars," in *A Notable Discovery of Coosnage* (London: T. N[elson], 1591); reprinted in Alexander B. Grosart (ed.), *The Life and Complete Works in Prose and Verse of Robert Greene, M.A.* (15 vols.; New York: Russell and Russell, 1964), X, 51 ff.

25. Thomas Deloney, *Thomas of Reading* (prob. London, 1598); reprinted in Merritt E. Lawlis (ed.), *The Novels of Thomas Deloney* (Bloomington: In-diana University Press, 1961), 285, from the edition of 1612. Both this and Greene's *Coosnage* are reprinted in Merritt Lawlis (ed.), *Elizabethan Prose Fic-tion* (New York: Odyssey, 1967).

26. Hooker, *Polity*, Bk. I, Chap. 7, p. 171.

Chapter VI

1. In the views that we find so incongruous Kepler was not unique. His achievement just makes his a dramatic case. Lynn Thorndike recalls that Michael Maestlin and Tycho Brahe were at once advanced astronomers and credulous astrologers. He says, "The case of Maestlin shows that we cannot divide men into two camps with lines sharply drawn between them, but that we ever find all sorts of intermediate shadings and combinations of opinion." Lynn Thorndike, *A History of Magic and Experimental Science* (8 vols.; New York: Macmillan and Columbia University Press, 1941), VI, 81. Thorndike is not similarly tolerant of John Dee. See VI, 26.

2. Humbler men on the Continent also suffered. Lucilio Vanini, not much more a naturalist than less heroic souls, was burned as an atheist in Toulouse in 1619. See Thorndike, *Magic and Science*, VI, 560–73.

3. E. J. Dijksterhuis, *The Mechanization of the World Picture*, trans. C. Dikshoorn (Oxford: Clarendon Press, 1961).

4. Francis R. Johnson, in *Astronomical Thought in Renaissance England* (Baltimore: Johns Hopkins Press, 1937), 3 and 9, records a count of scientific items in the Pollard and Redgrave *Short Title Catalogue*. For the twenty years before 1595 Johnson's figures understate the facts. The rate was accelerating.

5. W. P. D. Wightman, *Science and the Renaissance* (2 vols.; Edinburgh: Oliver and Boyd, 1962). Wightman's bibliography only sporadically mentions books not found in Aberdeen, but the list suggests what was available to Eng-lishmen who attended *A Midsummer Night's Dream*.

6. These books on mathematics are listed in A. W. Pollard and G. R. Redgrave, compilers, *Short Title Catalogue of Books Printed in England, Scotland, and Ireland and of English Books Printed Abroad, 1475–1640*, (London: The Bibliographical Society, 1926). For an account of a less earthy mathematics in Renaissance Italy, including the revival of Greek mathematics, see Paul Lawrence Rose, "Humanist Libraries and Mathematics: The Italian Libraries of the Quattrocento," *Studies in the Renaissance*, XX (1973), 46–105.

7. H. Billingsley, *The Elements of Geometrie of . . . Euclide . . . Faithfully (Now First) Translated into the Englishe Toung*, With a . . . Praeface Made by M. I. Dee, Specifying the Chiefe Mathematical Sciences, What They Are, and Whereunto Commodious: Where, Also, Are Discovered Certaine New Secrets Mathematicall and Mechanicall (London: John Day, 1570). I have used a photographic print from the Henry E. Huntington Library, San Marino, Calif.

8. Wightman, *Science and the Renaissance*, II, 73, describes *epistolae* by Dee now at Aberdeen. Thorndike, *Magic and Science*, 268, describes other letter writers.

9. Robert Parsons, *A Conference About the Next Succession to the Crown of Ingland* (N.p.: R. Doleman, 1594; rpt. New York: Da Capo Press, 1972), Pt. 1, Chap. 1, pp. 5–6. Catholics had special reasons for alertness to the bonds that hold a community together.

10. Steven Guazzo, *The Civile Conversation of M. Steeven Guazzo, the First Three Books Translated by George Pettie, Anno 1581*, introd. Sir Edward Sullivan (2 vol.; London: Constable, 1925), I, 31. See also John L. Lievsay, *Stefano Guazzo and the English Renaissance, 1575–1675* (Chapel Hill: University of North Carolina Press, 1961).

11. Guazzo, *Civile Conversation*, 39.

12. J. Spedding, R. L. Ellis, D. D. Heath (eds.) *The Works of Francis Bacon* (1860–64; 15 vols.; Boston: Houghton Mifflin, n.d.), XII, 132.

13. Guazzo, *Civile Conversation*, 41.

14. John M. Ziman, *Public Knowledge: An Essay Concerning the Social Dimension of Science* (London: Cambridge University Press, 1968), 9.

15. E. G. R. Taylor, *Tudor Geography* (London: Methuen, 1930), Richard Deacon, *John Dee* (London: Muller, 1968), and Peter J. French, *John Dee: The World of an Elizabethan Magus* (London: Routledge and Paul, 1972), place Dee in the history of scientific thought and discuss his influence.

16. For treatments of "Sir Walter Rauley's Schoole of Atheisme" and *Love's Labour's Lost* see Frances A. Yates, *A Study of "Love's Labour's Lost"* (Cambridge: Cambridge University Press, 1936); O. J. Campbell, *"Love's Labour's Lost* Restudied," in Campbell *et al.*, *Studies in Shakespeare, Milton, and Donne*, University of Michigan Publications, Vol. I, ed. Eugene S. McCartney (New York: Macmillan, 1925); Muriel C. Bradbrook, *The School of Night: A Study in the Literary Relationships of Sir Walter Ralegh* (Cambridge: Cambridge University Press, 1936); and Rupert Taylor, *The Date of "Love's Labour's Lost"* (New York: Columbia University Press, 1932). See also Ernest A. Strathmann, *Sir Walter Ralegh: A Study in Elizabethan Skepticism* (New York: Columbia University Press, 1951).

17. W. W. Greg (ed.), *Gesta Grayorum*, (London: Oxford University Press, 1914), 34–35.

18. F. H. Anderson, *The Philosophy of Francis Bacon* (Chicago: University of Chicago Press, 1948), 12. The Latin original appears in Spedding, Ellis, and Heath (eds.), *Works of Francis Bacon*, VI, 449: "*ut quae ad ingeniorum correspondentias captandas et mentium areas purgandas pertinent, edantur in vul-*

gus et per ora volitent." James Stephens, in *Francis Bacon and the Style of Science* (Chicago: University of Chicago Press, 1975), lays a somewhat different emphasis but deals extensively with Bacon's concern.

19. James D. Watson, *The Double Helix* (New York: Atheneum, 1968).

20. Thorndike, *Magic and Science,* 269.

21. Marie Boas, *The Scientific Renaissance, 1450–1630* (New York: Harper and Row, 1962), 242–45.

22. The scientific implications of the Society are now little stressed, but see Henry Hallam, *Introduction to the Literature of Europe in the Fifteenth, Sixteenth, and Seventeenth Centuries* (4 vols.; New York: A. C. Armstrong, 1891), II, 351; C. R. Weld, *History of the Royal Society* (London: J. W. Parker, 1848), 15; William Stebbing, *Sir Walter Ralegh* (Oxford: Clarendon Press, 1891), 273.

23. Sir Humphrey Gilbert, *Queene Elizabethes Achademy,* Vol. VIII in F. J. Furnivall (ed.), Early English Text Society, Extra Series, VIII (London: N. Trubner, 1869), 6.

24. Johnson, *Astronomical Thought,* 198–205. Johnson corrects the account in the *Dictionary of National Biography.* See also Francis R. Johnson, "Thomas Hood's Inaugural Address as Mathematical Lecturer of the City of London (1588)," *Journal of the History of Ideas,* III (1942), 94–106.

25. See John Burnet, *Early Greek Philosophy* (London: A. and C. Black, 1908), 52 ff. Bruno taught the plurality of worlds; he owed much to Nicholas of Cusa and was in sympathy with Thomas Digges.

26. As in Diogenes Laertius, *The Lives and Opinions of Eminent Philosophers,* trans. C. D. Yonge (London: H. G. Bohn, 1909), 435. The Greek word is *prolepsis.*

27. Guillaume du Bartas, *La Sepmaine,* enjoyed a reactionary popularity and some English translations years before Sylvester's rendering in 1598.

28. Thomas Henry Huxley, "William Harvey," *Fortnightly Review,* n.s., XXIII (1878), 175.

29. Alfred North Whitehead, *Science and the Modern World* (New York: Macmillan, 1950), 15–16.

30. For evidence suggesting proto-clock-works in the Greece of Archimedes and later, see Derek J. de Solla Price, *Science Since Babylon* (New Haven: Yale University Press, 1961), 36–44.

31. For a philosophical discussion of conversation in human development see George H. Mead, *Mind, Self, and Society* (Chicago: University of Chicago Press, 1962).

32. A. R. Hall, *The Scientific Revolution, 1500–1800* (Boston: Beacon Press, 1956), 84–86.

33. Michael Polanyi, *Personal Knowledge* (Chicago: University of Chicago Press, 1958), 132 ff. Polanyi quotes Kepler's exultat at length (p. 7). I have not seen a colleague streak naked and yelling across the campus or gush unrestrainedly like Kepler, but when one of them witnesses a previously unrecorded instructive bit of behavior in orchid, turtle, or Jupiter, he rejoices.

34. Arnold's lecture, widely accessible, is reprinted in Matthew Arnold, *On the Classical Tradition* (Ann Arbor: University of Michigan Press, 1960), Vol. I of Robert Henry Super (ed.), *The Complete Prose Works of Matthew Arnold* (9 vols.; Ann Arbor: University of Michigan Press, 1960).

Chapter VII

1. From the definition of naturalism in B. A. G. Fuller, *A History of An-*

cient and Medieval Philosophy (3rd ed.; Rev. by S. M. McMurrin; New York: Holt, Rinehart and Winston, 1955), Appendix VI, p. xlii.

2. It is not strange that academic people should praise the reasoning mind. Darwinian George H. Mead, however, has described mind modestly. Far from governing the universe, mind, he says, grew when certain organisms endured an accidental and perhaps temporary environmental situation because they happened to have it. George H. Mead, *Mind, Self, and Society* (Chicago: University of Chicago Press, 1962).

3. Edward Capell (ed.), in *Mr. William Shakespeare, His Comedies, Histories and Tragedies* (10 vols.; London: J. and R. Tonson, 1767), II, 116a, makes the following note, duly recorded with minor changes in the Furness *Variorum*, X, 220: "This 'Limander' should be Paris, by the lady he is coupl'd with: and he is call'd by his other name, Alexander, corrupted to Alisander (as in *Love's Lab. L.* V, ii, 567, et seq.) and Lisander, which master Bottom may be allow'd to make Limander of." I have been unable to find "Lisander" for "Alexander" unless in *A Midsummer Night's Dream* itself, where I take it "Lysander" (spelled just as commonly "Lisander" in the Quarto, of course) is indeed a form designed to put audiences in mind of Alexandros.

Often quoted is Dr. Johnson's recapture of what Bottom misspoke: "Limander and Helen, are spoken by the blundering player, for Leander and Hero." James Boswell the Younger (ed.), *The Plays and Poems of William Shakespeare* (21 vols.; London: F. C. and J. Rivington, 1821), V, 323. Capell's version of the "Limander" blunder makes a more fitting and provocative allusion than Johnson's, and it depends on a less violent departure from original forms: "Limander" is as far from "Alisander" as from "Leander," but "Helena" is much closer to "Helen" than to "Hero."

4. A lost retelling of the Cephalus and Procris story by Henry Chute, so Malone says, apparently had just been published when *A Midsummer Night's Dream* was first performed. So reports Horace Howard Furness (ed.), *A New Variorum Edition of Shakespeare* (24 vols.; Philadelphia: Lippincott, 1895), X, 220. But the story was already familiar in Ovid, *Metamorphoses* (Loeb Classical Library ed.; 2 vols.; London: William Heinemann, 1921), Vol. I, Bk. VII.

5. Northrop Frye, "The Argument of Comedy," in Alan Downer (ed.), *English Institute Essays* (New York: Columbia University Press, 1949), and often reprinted.

Chapter VIII

1. A major book about citizens is Louis B. Wright, *Middle-Class Culture in Elizabethan England* (Chapel Hill: University of North Carolina Press, 1935). See also A. L. Rowse, *The England of Elizabeth: The Structure of Society* (New York: Macmillan, 1951), esp. 107–260.

2. Widely read are books like Jack H. Adamson and H. F. Folland, *The Shepherd of the Ocean: An Account of Sir Walter Raleigh and His Times* (Boston: Gambit, 1969), and Lytton Strachey, *Elizabeth and Essex* (New York: Harcourt Brace, 1928).

3. See Sylvia L. Thrupp, *The Merchant Class of Medieval London, 1300–1500* (Chicago: University of Chicago Press, 1948), 2–5. W. K. Jordan, *The Charities of London, 1480–1660* (New York: Russell Sage Foundation, 1960), 47 ff., describes merchants' wealth and family origins.

4. A. R. Waller and Arnold Glover (eds.), *The Collected Works of William Hazlitt* (12 vols.; London: J. M. Dent, 1902), I, 244.

5. George Unwin, *Industrial Organization in the Sixteenth and Seventeenth Centuries* (Oxford: Clarendon Press, 1904), 5.

6. *Ibid.*, esp. 103–25. On page 107 Unwin says: "Most, if not all, of those London companies which were connected at the time of Elizabeth with the larger industries . . . [were] almost as far removed from the pure handicraft system on the one hand as . . . from the factory system on the other. The governing bodies of these companies, if not exclusively composed of traders, were dominated by the trading interest; but they were bound by their charter and ordinances to maintain the protective regulations which were the product of the handicraft tradition." See also Jordan, *Charities of London*, 51, on the fluidity of the citizen ranks, with ease of entry from below and exit upwards.

7. Robert J. Blackham, in *The Soul of the City: London's Livery Companies* (London: Sampson Low, n.d. [ca. 1931], tells the story. He says of Osborne's family (p. 102) that its "present head is the Duke of Leeds."

8. The story appears in the *Dictionary of National Biography*, XVIII, 765–66. If you ever visit St. Helen's within Bishopsgate you may see a magnificent tomb with recumbent figures of Sir John and his wife and a small figure of his daughter praying.

9. Douglas Bush, *English Literature in the Earlier Seventeenth Century* (Oxford: Clarendon Press, 1945), 12.

10. The uses of sea power were well known as early as Chaucer's Merchant. William Woodruff, in *Impact of Western Man: A Study of Europe's Role in the World Economy* (London: Macmillan, 1967), records European businessmen's later conquests.

11. This may be disputed. Getting in debt to the mercers was a vice of fashionable young men, and those who loved young men sometimes lost no love on the mercers.

12. Scholars have noticed almanacs in various ways. See for example, the quotation from Charles Knight in William Shakespeare, *A Midsummer Night's Dream*, The Arden Shakespeare, ed. Henry Cuningham (London: Methuen, 1905), 70.

13. Unconventional writers like Montaigne, as in *An Apology for Raymond Sebond*, also joined in reiterating sense fallibility.

14. Bush, *English Literature in the Earlier Seventeenth Century*, 26, wittily phrases the learned man's still strong preference: "The stationers would not hear of a psychological treatise in Latin, so that Burton was compelled to prostitute his muse in English."

15. See Faye Kelly, *Prayer in Sixteenth Century England* (Gainesville: University of Florida Press, 1966).

16. Everyone remembers John Shakespeare's status in Stratford. Wright, *Middle-Class Culture*, 18–19, lists other writers with middle-class fathers. The elder John Marlowe was a cobbler, James Peele a salter, Christopher Monday a draper, John Webster a merchant tailor, Robert Chettle a dyer, Nicholas Herrick a goldsmith, John Harvey a ropemaker, Robert Sylvester a clothier, John Donne an ironmonger, Thomas Browne a mercer. Thomas Deloney himself continued in the trade of silk weaver, but it would be absurd to make him the model for Bottom.

17. Robert Norman's *The Newe Attractive* was first published in London, 1581. I have used an Ann Arbor, Mich., University Microfilm of the edition "Newly corrected and amended by M. W. B.," London, 1585. For a discussion of Norman's place in scientific history see Edgar Zilsel, "The Origins of Gilbert's Scientific Method," in Philip P. Wiener and Aaron Noland (eds.), *Roots of Scientific Thought* (New York: Basic Books, 1957), 219–50, esp. 237–50.

18. Thomas J. J. Altizer and William Hamilton, *Radical Theology and the Death of God* (Indianapolis: Bobbs-Merrill, 1966), had a hearing for several years.

19. See Marjorie Nicolson, *The Breaking of the Circle* (Rev. ed.; New York: Columbia University Press, 1960), Chap. 3.

20. F. H. Anderson, in *The Philosophy of Francis Bacon* (Chicago: University of Chicago Press, 1948), 50, to indicate a fashion in thought, points out that "between the years 1475 and 1640 some sixty titles . . . of . . . St. Augustine were published in England, and during the same period . . . not a work of Aristotelian Thomas Aquinas." Of course Aquinas continued available in continental editions and there are other evidences of his persisting influence. Anderson reviews Bacon's anti-Aristotelian utterances in Chap. 6, 190–216.

21. Quoted by Rowse, *The England of Elizabeth*, 224.

22. See for example, in the translation of *The New Organon*, "The Second Book of Aphorisms," J. Spedding, R. L. Ellis, and D. D. Heath (eds.), *The Works of Francis Bacon* (1860–64; vols., Boston: Houghton Mifflin, n.d.), VIII, 181–210; Anderson, *The Philosophy of Francis Bacon*, 220; and W. A. Sessions, "Francis Bacon and the Negative Instance," *Renaissance Papers, 1970* (Durham, N.C.: Southeastern Renaissance Conference, 1971), 1–10.

23. Wright, in *Middle-Class Culture*, 595–96, speaks of applied science:
The Elizabethan public shows, toward the end of the sixteenth century, an unusual curiosity about inventions. Mechanical skill was developing and ingenious minds were striving to perfect useful devices. . . . Sir Hugh Platt, son of a wealthy London brewer . . . turned a hand to describing inventions [in] *The Jewell House of Art and Nature* (1594). . . . Scientific learning should find some practical outlet, he believes, and he vigorously attacks pedantic scientists who wrap their learning in too much Latin, or merely write of vague theories spun out of their studies and not from their practice. . . . Platt's zeal for applied science is obvious in his book, which teaches a curious variety of things: . . . how to use secret ink, how to make a wind vane which will register in the merchant's room in order that he may know at any hour whether winds are favorable, how to stain new walnut like old, how to cement broken glass, and scores of other useful processes.

24. G. H. Baillie, *et al.*, *Britten's Old Clocks and Watches and Their Makers* (London: E. and F. N. Spon, 1956), 7–8. The first Strasbourg clock of 1354 "consisted of a calendar, representing in a painting some indications relative to the principal movable feasts. In the middle part there was an astrolabe, whose pointers showed the movement of the sun and moon, the hours and their subdivisions. There was placed at the same elevation the prime mover, and the other wheelwork which caused the clock to go. The upper compartment was adorned with a statuette of the Virgin before whom, at noon, the three Magi bowed themselves. A cock placed upon the crown of the case crowed at the same moment, moving its beak and flapping its wings. A small set of chimes, composed of several cymbals, was also incorporated in the work."

25. Notice also Mercutio's ribald sentence about the dial's hand in *Romeo and Juliet*, II, iv, 118–19. Human acts also suggested automata that imitated human acts. When Richard likens insistent Buckingham to a Jack, he called to mind iron figures of men swinging hammers against bells to strike the hours, *Richard III*, IV, ii, 117.

26. Quotations from Rabelais, *Gargantua and Pantagruel* (Bk. I, Chap. 24), and *Vives: On Education*, trans. Foster Watson (Cambridge: Cambridge University Press, 1913), 208–209, appear in Walter E. Houghton, Jr., "The History

of Trades: Its Relation to Seventeenth Century Thought," in Wiener and Noland (eds.), *Roots of Scientific Thought,* 354–55.

27. Houghton documents the point in "History of Trades," 356–57.

28. The story is told by Francis R. Johnson, "Gresham College, Precursor of
the Royal Society," in Wiener and Noland (eds.), *Roots of Scientific Thought,*
328–53, and by F. R. Salter, *Sir Thomas Gresham* (London: L. Parsons, 1925).

29. Johnson, in "Gresham College," presents the evidence.

30. Wright, *Middle-Class Culture,* 65, quoting from Foster Watson, *The
Beginnings of the Teaching of Modern Subjects in England* (London: I. Pitman,
1909), xxxviii–xxxix.

Chapter IX

1. In Werner Heisenberg, *Physics and Philosophy: The Revolution in
Modern Science,* ed. Ruth Nanda Anshen, World Perspectives Series, XIX (New
York: Harper, 1958).

2. A resume of recent astronomy is William J. Kaufmann, *Relativity and
Cosmology* (New York: Harper and Row, 1973).

3. Alfred North Whitehead, *Science and the Modern World* (New York:
Macmillan, 1950), 65.

4. Bacon's *Advancement of Learning* and *Novum Organum* could not have
been in the memories of first audiences. But it appears likely that by 1595
Bacon had developed as much of his method as I have here summarized and
that it was being talked about among many of his contemporaries in London.
His fully developed "new method of science" is described by F. H. Anderson, in
The Philosophy of Francis Bacon (Chicago: University of Chicago Press, 1948)
especially 186–89 and 217 ff. A recent panegyric is Loren Eiseley, *The Man
Who Saw Through Time* (New York: Charles Scribner's Sons, 1973).

Thomas Henry Huxley has pointed out that inductive reasoning antedated
Bacon, asserting that Bacon neither exemplified nor adequately described the
fruitful processes of scientific thought. Albert S. Cook's introduction to his
edition of *The Advancement of Learning, Book I* (Boston: Ginn, 1904), xxix–
xxx, quotes from the article on William Harvey in *Fortnightly Review.* Despite
differences, in their proclaimed ways of thinking about the phenomenal world
Bacon, Briggs, Hariot, Harvey, William Gilbert, Robert Norman, John Dee, and
Thomas Digges were closer to one another and to the tacit assumptions and
mental procedures of leading London citizens making decisions about manufacture and commerce than any one of them was to John Donne in prayer.
People we are calling judicious playgoers were the intellectual community
(and of course it included Donne) in which these men could be understood. Not
everybody agrees with me: see R. G. Collingwood, *The Idea of History* (Oxford: Clarendon Press, 1946), Pt. II, Chap. 1.

5. This and the other English plays named below (Bale's *King John, The
Second Shepherds Play,* and the Brome *Abraham and Isaac*) are all reprinted in
John Matthews Manly (ed.), *Specimens of Pre-Shakespearean Drama* (2 vols.;
Boston: Ginn, 1897), I.

6. See William Empson, "Double Plots: Heroic and Pastoral in Main Plot
and Sub Plot," in his *Some Versions of Pastoral* (London: Chatto and Windus,
1935), 27; and Richard Levin, *The Multiple Plot in English Renaissance Drama*
(Chicago: University of Chicago Press, 1971), 10.

7. Among those who have found the double plot in *King Lear* irresistibly
stimulating are, of course, Empson, in "Double Plots," esp. 54, and Levin, in
The Multiple Plot, esp. 12–15.

Chapter X

1. As recently as H. Richard Niebuhr's *Radical Monotheism and Western Culture* (New York: Harper, 1960) a distinguished scholar has asserted that "Whatever is, is good," a dictum different from Pope's "Whatever is, is right." In alluding to Niebuhr I risk invoking a subtlety inappropriate to the deeply felt but not impeccable lay theology we are supposing for our playgoer, even though we give him not a little learning.

The impulse to construct worlds after the mind's imagining (if not the heart's desire), which I learned about from Shakespeare, Peter L. Berger learned from other sources. See his book *The Sacred Canopy* (Garden City, N.Y.: Doubleday, 1967), esp. Chap. 1.

2. Philip Sidney, *The Defence of Poesie*, ed. Albert Feuillerat (1595; Cambridge: Cambridge University Press, 1923), 28–29. Theseus is belittling not conscious liars but those whose minds give a new shape to the objects before their eyes. The first sentence of a letter, "The author to his loving cousin," prefaced to Robert Southwell's *Saint Peter's Complaint* (London: John Wolfe, 1595), because it fractionally duplicates a phrase in Theseus' speech, underscores Theseus' distinctive emphasis: "Poets, by abusing their talent and making the follies and fainings of love the customary subject of their base endeavors, have so discredited this faculty that a Poet, a Lover, and a Liar are by many reckoned but three words of one signification."

PRE-PERFORMANCE INDEX

This index is an inventory of books, plays, people, places, ideas, and other things demonstrably available to the memory of a playgoer who attended *A Midsummer Night's Dream* in 1595 and alluded to as bases for the understanding here presented. Omitted are such ever present items as England, London, and God.

Index

POST–1595 INDEX

Index, by author and title, to cited plays and writings appearing after 1595, and to writers after 1595 whose publications are not cited.

DATE DUE